"No one is a v   le or more
balanced stude   tri Trenin.
No one, anyw.   ussia? His
answer is, yes, but for reasons that are different and vastly
more complex than the reasons driving the discourse in the
West. US and European leaders will not get their policy toward
Russia right until they come to terms with the arguments in
this book."

**Robert Legvold, Columbia University, and author of _Return
to Cold War_**

"This rich and exceedingly well-written book considers whether
the impasse in relations between Russia and the West is due
to Putin's 'Realpolitik' or whether it reflects Putin's lack of
realism about Russia's true national interests. With Trenin, we
are in good hands. His lively analysis rewards its audience with
a stimulating reading and learning experience."

Jack Snyder, Columbia University

"Dmitri Trenin is one of the most lucid analysts of Russia
writing today. In this short but rich volume, he traces the recent
history of misguided policy and conflicts of interest that have
produced the current sharp deterioration in relations between
Russia and the West. A 'new normal' has emerged, he argues.
It is not a second Cold War but a period of new challenges and
opportunities, in which seeing Russia clearly is critical to peace
and security. To that end, there is no better place to start than
this present essay."

**Thomas Graham, Managing Director, Kissinger Associates,
and former Senior Director for Russia on the US National
Security Council staff**

Should We
Fear Russia?

Global Futures

Mohammed Ayoob, *Will the Middle East Implode?*
Christopher Coker, *Can War be Eliminated?*
Howard Davies, *Can Financial Markets be Controlled?*
Jonathan Fenby, *Will China Dominate the 21st Century?*
Andrew Gamble, *Can the Welfare State Survive?*
David Hulme, *Should Rich Nations Help the Poor?*
Joseph S. Nye Jr., *Is the American Century Over?*
Tamara Sonn, *Is Islam an Enemy of the West?*
Jan Zielonka, *Is the EU Doomed?*

Dmitri Trenin

———

Should We Fear Russia?

polity

First published in 2016 by Polity Press

Polity Press
65 Bridge Street
Cambridge CB2 1UR, UK

Polity Press
350 Main Street
Malden, MA 02148, USA

ISBN-13: 978-1-5095-1090-0
ISBN-13: 978-1-5095-1091-7 (pb)

A catalogue record for this book is available from the British Library.

Library of Congress Cataloging-in-Publication Data

Names: Trenin, Dmitri, author.
Title: Should we fear Russia? / Dmitri Trenin.
Description: Malden, MA : Polity Press, 2016. | Series: Global futures series | Includes bibliographical references.
Identifiers: LCCN 2016015429 (print) | LCCN 2016026584 (ebook) | ISBN 9781509510900 (hardback) | ISBN 9781509510917 (pbk.) | ISBN 9781509510931 (Mobi) | ISBN 9781509510948 (Epub)
Subjects: LCSH: Russia (Federation)--Foreign relations. | Russia (Federation)--Military policy. | Russia (Federation)--Foreign relations--Western countries. | Western countries--Foreign relations--Russia (Federation)
Classification: LCC JZ1616 .T74 2016 (print) | LCC JZ1616 (ebook) | DDC 327.47--dc23
LC record available at https://lccn.loc.gov/2016015429

Typeset in 11 on 15 Sabon by
Servis Filmsetting Ltd, Stockport, Cheshire
Printed and bound in Great Britain by CPI Group (UK) Ltd, Croydon

For further information on Polity, visit our website:
politybooks.com

Contents

Preface   vi

  Introduction   1
1 Analysis of Fears   22
2 The Russia Challenge   56
3 Bringing Russia into Line   76
4 Navigating the New Normal   98
  Conclusion: How Conflict with the West
  Impacts on Russia   116

Further Reading   122
Notes   124

Preface

Since early 2014, barely a day passes when manifestations of Russia's foreign policy assertiveness and military resurgence don't make the headlines in the Western world. After Ukraine and Syria, it became absolutely clear: Russia has not only broken out of the post-Cold War order in its former Soviet neighborhood but challenged that order elsewhere. Two things stand out in Moscow's recent actions: they caught a lot of people off guard, and they involved the use of force, sometimes in unorthodox ways. Thus, it is hardly surprising that the "Russia threat" is at the forefront of people's minds. So, should Russia be feared?

The "we" in the title, of course, refers to the readers, wherever they live – in the United States, Europe, Asia, the Middle East, or elsewhere – who have become – or have always been, to various degrees – concerned about Russia. I was born in Moscow and live within a couple of miles from the Kremlin, the source of other people's worries. And I pledge to you to give an honest answer to the question from inside the source of the perceived threat – no easy commission.

Many in Russia would scoff at the question, dismissing it as an example of Western paranoia, age-old Russophobia, a throwback to the Cold War, or a deliberate attempt at smearing Russia. Like most people anywhere, most ordinary Russians think of their country as essentially good, reasonably friendly, and essentially peace-loving – and, some will add, grossly misunderstood. Being able to look at one's country from a distance is a rare and poisoned gift.

More sophisticated Russians would explain that the present-day Russian Federation has no intention of changing the world according to her preferences, unlike its immediate predecessor, the Soviet Union – or, some would not resist the temptation of saying, present-day America. Moscow, they would argue, is now guided by its interests rather than by ideologies. Russia is no real democracy, but it is part of the global capitalist economy and lives in a global information space. Its citizens are free to travel, and many have seen other parts of the world, where no one is perfect. Bottom line: demonizing anyone serves no useful purpose.

"Realists" would point out that Russia is a post-imperial polity, in transit to a nation-state, and a great power; that it has a set of security interests that others need to take account of, whether they agree with them or not. Annexing Crimea, in their view, was a defensive move against the post-Cold War expansion of the West, and its legitimacy lies not so much in the legality of the annexation as in the genuine will of the bulk of the Crimean population to join Russia. To this group, Russia is an underdog power fighting for its survival as a major independent geopolitical entity against the far superior forces of its competitors.

Neither set of arguments finds many takers outside of Russia's borders. To a lot of its neighbors, Russia as a security problem still looms larger than life. Tsarist, communist or contemporary, it is still feared, and often hated. Those living in countries which are bigger, farther away and more self-confident face the uncomfortable reality of a Russia which is intensely feared by some of their partners and which itself actively challenges the order underpinned by their senior transatlantic ally, in whom they entrusted their security seven decades ago.

In the United States, of course, there is no deep

fear of Russia, deemed by the elite consensus a has-been power, now in terminal decline. In raw power terms, Russia is a midget compared to the US. Crucially, the fact that Russia, despite its many flaws and failings, remains a nuclear weapons peer of the United States and, as in the Cold War, practices nuclear deterrence toward the US, does not appear particularly threatening to Americans. Primitive North Korean systems and the non-existent Iranian ones raise much more concern in this regard. Despite the return of confrontation and the talk of Moscow's unpredictability, Russia is evidently considered a rational player, at least in the nuclear field.

Thoughtful Americans would instead point to the numerous vulnerabilities of present-day Russia: the economic, social, political and ideological underpinnings of the current Russian system are all very weak. They would recall that the country imploded twice in the twentieth century, with disastrous consequences for itself and powerful consequences, if very different each time, for others. Without a credible model of economic development and strong societal institutions, which are still absent, Russia may go down once again. If it does, implications for its neighbors will be severe and the impact on the rest of the world significant. Forget

Russian strength, they would urge, watch out for its weakness!

Indeed, Russia's insecurity is an issue. The current political system rests on the strong link between the leader, President Putin, and the bulk of the Russian people. Should that link be strained or severed, there is virtually no safety net. In 2015, the Kremlin's chief political adviser said that, "as long as there [was] Putin, there [would be] Russia" – dubious laudation, if taken literally. Many of the moneyed elite are self-centered and self-indulgent. Much of the officialdom is using their positions for self-enrichment on the job. Russian society and polity has not yet concluded peace with itself: the "us" (common people) vs. "them" (elites) division runs deep. Russia's conservatives, socialists and liberals are still dreaming of their own national hegemony and find little common ground, except, for most – after Crimea – in foreign policy.

Russia has not found peace with its near neighbors either. The Ukrainian conflict continues to smolder, Georgia is nervous, Poland and the Baltic States are openly hostile, and Turkey in November 2015 shot down a Russian warplane, causing a breakdown in the heretofore vibrant relations between the two. To the west, it faces a Europe where NATO has openly resumed its historical mission of containing

Russia; to the east, it sees a China that has risen to the point when it has decided to begin economic expansion in Eurasia, as part of the "One Belt, One Road" project. To the south, Russia watches with growing concern the expansion of Islamist radicalism and extremism, which it had hoped to check by means of a military operation in Syria.

The hard fact in 2016 is that Russia's relations with much of the rest of Europe are marked by mutual alienation, and its asymmetrical confrontation with the United States is both serious and dangerous. Partial convergence of Russian and Western interests in Syria cannot alter the fundamental clash of interests. Mutual hostility is palpable, and the chances of a direct collision between Russia and the United States are not negligible. The thick atmosphere of Russo-American rivalry, no matter how unequal, breeds even more mistrust, suspicion and fear. Even if the worst doesn't come to the worst, the effect will be significant, and lasting.

The Russia–Europe rift is particularly damaging to Russia, newly estranged from Europe. It isn't a welcome thing for Europe, either. For centuries, Russia was the "east of the West", an extension of Europe all the way to the Pacific. After the end of the Cold War, a prospect arose of a "greater

Europe" that would include Russia and would rest on a symbiosis of Russian resources and European technologies. What could happen, however, is a Russia as the "west of the East", dominated by China and embracing much of Eurasia. This would shift the geopolitical axis of the Eurasian continent precisely as it is becoming increasingly more intertwined.

The problem with Russia is that it doesn't fit neatly in one box. It is both strong and weak; authoritarian and lawless; traditionalist and valueless. Everything there may change overnight, and nothing will do so in two hundred years. No wonder that one can fear one's own past fears, dreading their comeback. Russia's imperial past and Stalin's long shadow have never quite left its neighbors' minds alone, even in the days of Russia dismantling its historical empire and shedding its worn communist clothes. Seen through these lenses, Putin looks just the last man in the long line going all the way back to Ivan the Terrible..

So much for the complexities of the question and for the difficulties of answering it, neither of which should be construed as an excuse for fudging the issue. I will attempt to address the question squarely, knowing full well that your interest in the answer is anything but academic. A short version sounds like this. Most fears about Russia are dated or groundless. At the same time, a lot of dangers linked to America's or Europe's relations with it are all too happily ignored. In other words: Russia should not be feared but, rather, always be handled with care. If you are interested in an answer which is a bit longer, you are welcome to read further.

Dmitri Trenin
Sergiev Posad, 8 February 2016

Introduction

The Ukraine crisis of 2014 drew a line under the quarter century of virtually unprecedented Russian–Western cooperation, which began with the end of the Cold War and Russia's shaking off communism. After events in Ukraine, in the view of a number of serious and seasoned observers, the Cold War has staged a comeback. These observers point to the new political front lines being drawn in Europe, this time in its eastern part rather than in the center of the continent. They see this new divide solidifying into a zone of military confrontation. They add that the values gap between the West and Russia is as real as the old ideological confrontation between liberal democracy and communism. Finally, with Russia aligning itself with China and Iran, as well as with authoritarian regimes from Belarus to Syria to Venezuela to Zimbabwe, there is an element of globalism in the new stand-off.

I, on the contrary, do not find the Cold War analogy very useful. Not so much because of the obvious differences between then and now – the absence of an iron curtain; the off-center rather than pivotal global importance of US–Russian relations compared to US–Soviet ones; or the much reduced salience of the ideological factor. As someone who vividly remembers the Cold War, I am concerned that analogies which are too close to that period in history can create patterns of thought that would be misleading and result in preventable mistakes. People would be preparing for things which would not happen, while missing those that would. The situation in Western–Russian relations now may be as bad, and as dangerous, as at any time during the Cold War, but it is bad and dangerous in its own new way.

The absence of an iron curtain makes information space a prime battlefield in the new competition between the Russian state-run propaganda and the Western mainstream media. The still largely open space makes this 24/7 battle extremely dynamic and particularly ruthless, with virtually no holds barred. Information is no longer suppressed, but it is difficult or sometimes impossible to tell truth from falsehood.

Introduction

Geo-economics, alongside information space, has become a key area of Russian–Western confrontation. Contrary to liberal expectations, interdependence – i.e., between Russia and the EU – has neither prevented nor dampened the conflict over Ukraine. If anything, interdependence made the rupture more painful than during the Cold War. Russia's integration into the global economy allows for a more effective use of Western economic sanctions in an effort to make the Kremlin change its course.

The obvious asymmetry in power and status between Russia and the United States leads Moscow to elect the field which it finds more comfortable – military action – and to put a premium on the swiftness and boldness of its own steps. The absence of a balance turns the rivalry into a competition of wills, where the Kremlin also capitalizes on the absolute dominance of the Russian president in the national decision-making process. And the values gap, unlike the ideological divide of the past, makes it virtually impossible for the United States, occupying in its own thinking the moral high ground, to reach a compromise with so unworthy an adversary. These are elements which make the current rivalry more fluid and less predictable than the Cold War stand-off.

Introduction

Whether one prefers to refer to the Cold War or not, one has to admit that mutual adversity between the West and Russia is the new normal, which is likely to last. Trust was not really achieved even in the period of cooperation, but deep distrust comes now with the utter lack of respect, not even of the kind sometimes accorded to an enemy. There is no element of balance either. The Soviet–Western competition is long over, with the West having declared itself the victor. To treat Russia as an equal would not only be wrong as a matter of fact; it would be wrong in moral terms and, whoever might do so, compromises the values of the West. Among the dangers facing the civilized world, US President Barack Obama famously put Russia somewhere between a contagious disease and a terrorist grouping.

This adversity is likely to continue beyond the lifetime of the Obama administration. The forty-fifth US president could actually be tougher on Russia than the forty-fourth one. One hears in Washington that pressure on Moscow will last at least as long as Vladimir Putin's reign in Russia – which may be a long wait. It is an interesting question what might happen if Russia, as some people hope, cracks under Western pressure and capitulates. If it does not, however, it is hard to imagine that Putin or a successor will roll back the Kremlin's policies enough to win a "normalization" of relations with the United States. There can be some provisional "fix" in Donbass, but there will be no return to the halcyon days of Russia's attempted integration into the West in the 1990s, or its equally unfulfilled ambition of forging alliances with the United States and NATO in the 2000s.

The current predicament in Russian–Western relations is anything but fortuitous. European history proves, rather convincingly, that a post-conflict failure to integrate a former enemy, particularly if it is a major power, or at least to make it feel secure and at ease, results in a new conflict roughly a generation away. The way World War I ended made World War II very likely. By contrast, post-World War II integration of West Germany into the US-led system of alliances and the European Common Market essentially resolved the "German Question" that had plagued Europe since the second half of the nineteenth century. With the Cold War being a conflict of a scale, intensity and duration – but not casualties, of course – comparable to a world war, the failure of Russia's Western integration, which was evident from the mid-2000s, bode ill. People were warned and should have been alarmed.

Things are never so simple, though, and any

historical analogies need to be taken with a huge grain of salt. One cardinal difference between post-World War II West Germany and post-Cold War Russia is that the Germans fully accepted US leadership and eagerly fitted into the US-led "free world" as *model pupils*, as the phrase went then. The Russians, on the contrary, after a very brief period of demonstrating their willingness to embrace US values and interests as their own, began to clamor for a co-equal position in the post-Cold War order, or at minimum for full recognition of their special security interests the way they themselves defined them. In other words, they demanded power-sharing at the top of the system, or at least special privileges within it.

Neither was, or could have been, on offer. Russia of the 1990s, as the prime successor to the Soviet Union, was, in realist terms, a defeated power in all but name; it was also exceedingly weak and seemingly growing weaker; and it was much nearer to the bottom than to the top of the post-communist democracy/market class. The more insightful Americans and Europeans soon concluded that Russia would not make a good – i.e., reliable – ally, in the image of Germany. If allowed into NATO, Russia would probably have undermined the American leadership by its outsize demands and its mischievous propensity to build coalitions against the US – with Germany, France and others. A keen sense of great-power sovereignty was still in the DNA of the Russian political class; the absence of a military defeat at the close of the Cold War – and, instead of post-conflict "re-education," the liberal talk of a "victory for all" – clouded and confused popular perceptions; and the enormity of the task of Russian modernization made Russia not only a hopeless but also an undesirable ally.

While Russia was turning out to be "beyond the pale," the West proceeded to build a "Europe whole and free" without Russia by expanding its principal institutions in the area, the North Atlantic Treaty Organization and the European Union. To the Clinton administration and liberal internationalists across the West, extending NATO and the EU east of the Cold War divide made a lot of sense, as the countries in the region were eager to accede to the West and, while in the process of accession, to adopt Western ways of doing things. Such integration was also the best way of preventing conflicts among the countries of Central and Eastern Europe.

As a result, by the late 2000s, virtually all of Europe outside the former Soviet Union had evolved into a single economic, political, security and humanitarian space. The oft-asked but never clearly answered question about the borders of Europe was being solved on the ground, not in the discussion fora. Russia's designated role was that of a partner of, not a party to, the expanded West.

To the Russian foreign and security policy community, such treatment was nothing less than insult added to injury. Some bemoaned the "Versailles-like" conditions allegedly imposed on Russia. Nearly all fulminated at the "perfidious" Western scheme of bringing NATO all the way to Russia's doorstep, supposedly in contravention of promises made by US and Western European leaders to Soviet president Mikhail Gorbachev at the time of Germany's reunification in 1990.

These Russian claims, however, rested on shaky foundations. Rather than being castigated and turned into a pariah à la post-Versailles Germany, Russia inherited the Soviet seat at the UN Security Council and all of the USSR's nuclear arsenal, joined the G7 (which thus became G8), the Council of Europe, and the World Trade Organization, and acquired privileged status as a partner of both NATO and the EU – all with the West's assistance. True, the Soviet Union's $100 billion debt to the West was not forgiven, unlike Poland's, but Russia was not saddled with reparations and retributions.

Moreover, having had – and been able – to pay its debt eventually saved Russia's pride.

Essentially, Russian grievances against its Western partners fall into two categories. The first one is mostly to do with the West's refusal to appreciate what Russia did to end the Cold War – from allowing Eastern Europe to "go its own way" to shaking off communism and dismantling the Soviet Union at home – together with its failure to integrate Russia into its midst and to give it an elevated status there. The other one reproaches the West for its refusal to treat Russia as a great power in its own right, complete with a sphere of interests around its borders, and immune from Western interference in its own affairs. Both sets of grievances misread the nature of international relations.

The Russian complainers ignore the hard fact that the Soviet Union utterly lost the economic, ideological and political competition with the West and that, instead of the "convergence" of the two systems, as Andrei Sakharov and many other intellectuals had hoped, and a sort of "bi-hegemony" of Moscow and Washington, as Gorbachev's advisers anticipated, the West celebrated a complete and total victory and the United States entered a period of global dominance unprecedented in history. In the final stages of the Cold War, Moscow gave in to Washington's demands not only in the issues of arms control and geopolitics but also in human rights, economic freedoms and the treatment of the Baltic republics. Russians demanded recognition for their seemingly graceful but actually painful exit from communism and the empire and claimed a status no longer supported by the realities at hand, but these things could not have been had for the asking.

The United States and its allies were fully triumphant. Robert Gates, then CIA director, called his drive into the Kremlin in 1992 for talks a "victory lap." He later reflected that

> [F]rom 1993 onward, the West, and particularly the United States, [had] badly underestimated the magnitude of Russian humiliation in losing the Cold War and then in dissolution of the Soviet Union, which amounted to the end of the centuries-old Russian Empire. The arrogance, after the collapse, of American government officials, academicians, businessmen, and politicians in telling the Russians how to conduct their domestic and international affairs (not to mention the internal psychological impact of their precipitous fall from superpower status) had led to deep and long-term resentment and bitterness.[1]

The end of the Cold War, however, signaled more the defeat of the Soviet system, which had become unsustainable in a number of key areas, starting from economics, than a victory for the West. The defeat of the system was mainly the work of the Russian elites and people, who, alongside others – Armenians, Balts, Georgians, Ukrainians – opened a new beginning for themselves, although at a high price. The fact that the metropolitan territory of an empire led the way out of it is a rare occurrence in world history.

To blame the West for the downfall of the USSR is factually wrong. US President George H. W. Bush's July 1991 speech in Kiev, in which he urged the Ukrainians to remain in the Soviet Union, revealed the keen understanding in Washington of the dangers inherent in a collapse of a nuclear superpower. The utterly false claims of US responsibility for the disintegration of the USSR put Russians into the position of fake victims, while diminishing their twin historical accomplishments – or responsibility, depending on where one stands on these issues – for a peaceful end to the seven decades of communist dictatorship and a voluntary dissolution of the 300-year-old empire.

As for the NATO argument, the West's mistake was not that its leaders had broken any formal commitments – which were non-existent – or informal promises – which were exceedingly vague and widely open to interpretation – to their Soviet counterpart, but that it lacked a credible strategy toward a major power left outside of its expanding alliances and feeling the discomfort of it, to say the least. This discomfort could be papered over, managed and minimized, but eventually it led to a sudden pushback.

With hindsight, some senior Western statesmen concede that, in the words of Robert Gates, "moving so quickly after the collapse of the Soviet Union to incorporate so many of its formerly subjugated states into NATO was a mistake." To Gates, "NATO expansion was a political act, not a carefully considered military commitment, thus undermining the purpose of the alliance and recklessly ignoring what the Russian considered their own vital national interests."[2] However, this realist assessment was a minority view at the time of making decisions about NATO's enlargement.

Essentially, the failure to understand the consequences of expanding the NATO security area while leaving Russia outside it was rooted in the widely held belief that the "end of history" had arrived: that classical geopolitics no longer applied in the globalized world, that, in the post-Cold War environment, compromising with authoritarian regimes, especially about third parties, meant compromising one's own core principles, and that anyway Russia was on a declining path. Conventional wisdom suggested that Russia had no option but to take the world as it is, and adjust to it, by bandwagoning on the West.

This, however, was not the way things looked from the Kremlin. In his 2007 speech to the Munich Security Conference, President Putin strongly denounced US post-Cold War global dominance and vowed to resist it. The five-day war between Russia and Georgia in 2008 sent a chilling message that the safe limits of NATO's enlargement to the east had been reached. The reset in US–Russian relations which followed in 2009–10 during Barack Obama's first presidential term was useful, but shallow and non-strategic – thus reversible. At the same time, the power of Russian patriotism and nationalism, subdued and suppressed in the first post-Cold War decade, began to surge. Vladimir Putin became its standard bearer, seeking to consolidate both his hold on power and the unity of the country at large.

The relationship with the United States meanwhile stagnated, and then began rapidly to deteriorate. In 2014, push came to shove. A conflict broke out over Ukraine, which, in the words of Robert Gates, was a "monumental provocation" to Moscow. Historical connections between Russia and Ukraine, going back over a thousand years, were ignored; Russian Foreign Minister Sergei Lavrov's warnings that US support for regime change in Kiev would destroy US–Russian relations were brushed off.[3] The US–Russian showdown could have happened in a different place and at a different moment, but the fact that it occurred over a country which was so important for Russia made it certain that it would be very serious, very painful, and last a very long time.

The Ukraine crisis was not the first war in Europe after the fall of the Berlin Wall. In 1999, NATO air forces bombed Yugoslavia, including Belgrade, for seventy-eight days to make the Serbian leader Slobodan Milošević back down in Kosovo, a majority-Albanian province which as a result proclaimed independence. The Kosovo crisis was preceded by three years of war in neighboring Bosnia, which claimed 200,000 lives, and which also saw NATO aerial engagements on behalf of the Croats and Muslims and against the Serbs. The Balkan conflicts, however, were safely insulated: they were fought by the locals, managed by the West, and – because of Russia's material weakness and its still continuing effort at adjustment to the new realities – did not lead to a great-power stand-off. Europe was burning at the edges but felt basically safe, having had to cope only with the stream of refugees, which seems small and orderly by today's standards.

Ukraine, fifteen years later, was different. Russia proceeded swiftly first to secure the Crimean peninsula, help stage a popular referendum there, and then to annex it. The success of the Russian military operation stunned outside observers. The enlargement of Russian territory evoked neighbors' memories of the past. Using the techniques dubbed hybrid warfare by the Western media, Russia supported an armed rebellion in the Donbass region in the east of Ukraine and prevented Kiev from crushing it.

By sending its warplanes close to NATO countries' borders, and allowing them to fly close to Western aircraft and ships, Russia sent a clear message to Western countries that, unlike in the Balkan wars, they would not be able to sit it out and watch Slavs kill one another. In the event of an escalation of the conflict, the Kremlin appeared to be saying, NATO countries too would be affected. To make the message even clearer, Putin publicly mentioned later that he had been considering putting Russia's nuclear weapons on high alert. Russia and the West came closer to a head-on collision than had been the case in at least three decades: 2014 was the most dangerous year in Europe since the 1983 Able

Archer exercise, if not since the 1962 Cuban missile crisis.

2015 put a freeze on the conflict in Donbass, which reduced the dangers of dangerous escalation but made the Russia–NATO stand-off permanent. Following the Wales summit of September 2014, NATO's contingency planning was revised to take account of a Russia now seen as hostile. Western and Russian forces began to exercise close to each other's territory, and NATO's eastern members – Poland, the Baltic States and Romania – received token Western troop deployments and some heavy weapons. The NATO secretary general's 2016 annual report referred to resurgent Russia as a major security challenge to the alliance. Senior US military commanders and defense officials began to refer to Russia as an adversary, which soon became routine. Ashton Carter, the US defense secretary, named Russia as the number one security issue to the United States, ahead of China, North Korea, Iran and ISIL.[4]

On the Russian side, there was no dispute as to who was the principal adversary. The National Security Concept adopted on New Year's Eve 2016 referred to the US and NATO actions as a security threat. To the Russian General Staff, however, the "moment of truth" about the United States and other nominal Western partners had already taken place years ago, over Kosovo.

In 2015, Russia made another step to challenge the US-led order by intervening militarily in Syria and hitting in the process some of the groups supported by the United States and its allies. The Russians not only broke the US monopoly on global military intervention. By inserting themselves in the midst of a war which had already involved a US-led coalition, they complicated the Western operations in Syria and Iraq, made common cause with Iran, raised the prospect of a war by proxy, briefly evoked the possibility of a quasi-alliance with France, caused a political collision with Ankara when Turkey downed a Russian bomber, and forced Washington to treat Moscow as an indispensable party to both the war and peace in Syria. Forcing his way to the high table, and making others deal with him out of necessity if not of choice, has become Vladimir Putin's diplomatic trademark in his relations with US leaders.

This combative foreign policy is being waged against the background of an unmistakably authoritarian Russian domestic regime, which prides itself in following the conservative tradition and publicly rejects some of the latter-day European values, particularly on the issues of gay rights, family, religion, migration, and the role of the state. It is supported by a competent and effective information/propaganda apparatus that contributes to the massive approval of Putin's ratings at home and reaches out beyond Russia's borders. Even though Russia's global popularity is low, which is hardly surprising given Western global information dominance, some of Moscow's themes find an audible echo in many parts of the world, from China to Latin America to the Middle East to Europe.

So, a blunt and cheerful "no" to the question in the title of this book looks both naïve and irresponsible. Surely, adversarial relations with a major power always carry risks. If the country in question is a major military power, with a huge nuclear arsenal, the risks are so much higher. If it is an authoritarian country whose decision-making is ultra-centralized and secretive, whose policies are sometimes hard to read, and whose actions are designed to catch others off guard, anxieties can turn to fears. This is precisely Russia's image in the public mind. Fear, however, is a poor guide to sound policies, or even to proper understanding. Fear could also be a problem in itself.

I begin this book with an analysis of existing Russia-related fears: their causes, their roots and their rationality. I will examine closely the things which make Westerners fear Russia and try to assess the proper dimensions of the factors behind the concerns, anxieties and worries. The conclusion from the opening chapter, I can tell even now, is that, while most fears need to be put to rest, the Russian challenge to the US-dominated/led world order is real, serious and long term.

The next stage will be to explore the nature of the Russian challenge. What is Russia really up to in its neighborhood and beyond – e.g., in the Middle East? What is it that its leader and elites want? To what extent is Russia's foreign policy a mere tool of the Kremlin's regime preservation, as some, including in Russia, claim? Other key questions include: How much does Russia's challenge matter to the United States and Europe, in the global scheme of things? And can Russia sustain it? The author's answer to the last question is probably "yes", and that both Russia and the challenge it is posing to the current US-dominated global system should not be discounted.

This leads to the logical question of dealing with the challenge. There have been efforts at consolidating allies and partners, isolating and sanctioning Russia, helping Beijing keep a distance from Moscow, and countering the Kremlin propaganda. How effective have these been? What is the outlook for these essentially punitive policies? What chances of success does the hardline approach – keep the pressure on until Moscow's will breaks – have? Compared to that, do the pragmatists stand a better chance of getting a satisfactory arrangement? Various scenarios will be offered.

Since the stand-off is serious, how can the risks be reduced? What confidence-building measures need to be taken? What channels of communication need to be used to send and receive messages without danger of a fateful misunderstanding? While accommodation with Russia will carry a cost that few in the West today, particularly the United States, are prepared to pay, is some modus vivendi with Russia possible? How to be able jointly to oppose Islamist extremism, terrorism, and WMD proliferation while continuing to live in the wider environment of confrontation?

Finally, what about the Russians themselves? How do they see their place and role in the twenty-first-century world? How genuine and how permanent is their shift to Asia? In the emerging Greater Eurasia, from the Pacific to the Atlantic, is Russia the east of the West, or is it becoming the west of the East, and does this matter at all? What would a future relationship with the United States and the European Union look like from a Russian perspective? How would that fit into the general universe of Moscow's foreign policy? Should the Russians fear the West?

1

Analysis of Fears

Fears of Russia in the West predate the Cold War (1947), the formation of the Red Army (1918) and the Bolshevik revolution (1917). A good summary of them could be found in an article by Frederick Engels in 1890, "The Foreign Policy of Russian Tsarism."[5] To Engels and his colleague Karl Marx, the principal source of fear was the expansionist nature of the Russian state, which, in its quest for hegemony in Europe and Asia, devoured some of its neighbors and subjugated others. Russia's rampant expansionism was made even more repugnant by the authoritarian and repressive character of its domestic regime.

This view from the West has not changed much, despite the peaceful toppling of the communist system by the Russian people in August 1991 and the unprecedented voluntary dismantlement of the historical Soviet/Russian empire in 1989–91. This process was not only led by Moscow, which accepted that 25 million ethnic Russians would be left outside the Russian Federation, it also drastically reduced the country's armed forces and scaled back the defense industry. Today, the Russian state often continues to be credited with an "essentially predatory nature," with a clear "preference to squeezing foreign countries to patient construction at home."[6]

Imperial revival

Just before Hillary Clinton stepped down as US secretary of state at the start of Barack Obama's second term, she called Vladimir Putin's project of a Eurasian Union an attempt to restore the Soviet Union. Beneath the veneer of "regional integration," Putin's goals, in her view, were "rebuilding a lost empire" and "re-Sovietizing" the Russian periphery; his method, like that of his predecessors, was "always testing, and pushing one's boundaries."[7]

Whether Putin was aiming at a new edition of the empire or at some loosely defined Moscow-led "power center in Eurasia," one thing was clear. After a brief delusion in the early 1990s when

Russia's foreign minister confided in a former US president, who was stunned by the confession, that Russia did not have interests that differed from the common interests of the democratic West, Moscow has learned not only to define its own interests but also to assert them. The most vital of these interests have always been concentrated in the territory of the former Soviet Union.

Russia's break with its empire was not immediately considered as final. As far back as 1994 Henry Kissinger warned about the risk of the "re-imperialization" of Russia.[8] The very use of such an unwieldy term suggests that it was carefully chosen. The United States, with a long history of helping others – starting with the British – divest themselves of their colonial possessions, was clearly pursuing the same policy with regard to post-Soviet Russia. It was one thing for George H. W. Bush to fear the collapse of a nuclear superpower; once the division of the Soviet Union became official, and its nukes were secured, Washington became a supporter of the new states' genuine independence from the Russian Federation. Moscow's initial instinct to treat its ex-borderlands as something not-quite-foreign, captured in the phrase "near abroad," immediately became suspicious and had to be resisted.

Analysis of Fears

The new states themselves, for their part, sought to rely on US and, to a lesser degree, European support to protect their independence, which still looked too fragile. The West leaned hard on Moscow to make sure that the Russian forces left the Baltic States by 1994. By that year, the last remaining Russian garrisons had left Germany and Eastern Europe. Once their departure was completed, the Russian military presence in Europe, in geographical terms, reached its lowest ebb in three centuries. Moreover, almost immediately, the opposite tide began, as Poland, Hungary and the Czech Republic applied in the same year to join NATO. To many Russians, this was zero-sum at its starkest: even as Russia's power was receding, it was being replaced by the expanding power of the West. No vacuum, no middle ground was allowed to exist. When Moscow began to protest against NATO's eastern enlargement, however, these protests were interpreted by the West as imperial nostalgia, another cause for concern.

Meanwhile, other fears arose as some of the former Soviet republics experienced ethnic separatism. In newly independent Moldova and Georgia, separatist groups have come to rely on the military protection of the Russian army garrisons and political and economic support from Moscow.

Even though ad hoc peacekeeping arrangements were reached soon after initial clashes, Russian forces in Transnistria, Abkhazia and South Ossetia were regarded by Chisinau and Tbilisi as occupiers, impinging on their newborn sovereignty and threatening their independence. To those with long memories, the Russian Federation was clawing back the territories of the former Soviet Union, much like Soviet Russia in 1918–20 was "reintegrating" the former imperial borderlands, snuffing out their short-lived independence. Thus, the most serious fear of Russia is that of Russian imperialism.

Use of force

A major contributor to the fear factor is the Kremlin's willingness to use military force, starting in the Russian North Caucasus in the 1990s and the early 2000s against local separatists turned extremists, which many in the West chose to see in terms of a colonial power fighting a national liberation movement. "The Kremlin has shown," said the historian Norman Davies, "that it is quite prepared to use armed force; the West has shown that it is not." Davies meant, not against Russia: US and other Western militaries had been consistently using force since the early 1990s. The problem, of course, was the practical impossibility of attacking a nuclear superpower. This, in Davies's view, "creates an asymmetrical relationship with Russia, militarily weak but mentally decisive, which can expect to get almost anything it wants."[9] Although this is obviously an overstatement, it points to a key problem: for all its military superiority that it has been using elsewhere quite liberally, the United States lacks serious military options vis-à-vis Russia.

One thing Vladimir Putin has learned from the history of both Gorbachev's and Yeltsin's dealings with the West, is never to be weak, and never to appear weak. "The weak get beaten." Even if the odds are against Russia, Putin is punching above the country's weight rather than submitting himself to the will of others. Over time, Putin went further. Summing up his own experience of fifteen years at the helm of the Russian state, he concluded that, if a fight is inevitable, one needs to strike first. Looking from the Kremlin, over the years Russia had drawn a number of red lines to its partners, which they chose to ignore. Finally, this provoked Moscow's pushback. In Putin's view, his predecessors' main mistake was not being assertive enough in defending the country's national interests.

These red lines, first drawn by Foreign Minister

Yevgeny Primakov in 1996, referred to the issue of admitting ex-members of the Warsaw Pact, which had formed the Soviet Union's strategic glacis in Europe, to NATO. The combination of Russian opposition to NATO's enlargement and its support for self-proclaimed separatist states led in 2008 to the first large-scale use of Russian military power since the demise of the Soviet Union. The Russian forces were brought into action by the botched attempt by the impetuous Georgian president Mikheil Saakashvili to re-establish control over the rebel region of South Ossetia, which led to the killing of a number of Russian peacekeepers there.

Once the war began, Russian troops did not confine themselves to the immediate area of conflict but proceeded to occupy areas of Georgia proper, coming within a striking distance of the Georgian capital Tbilisi. The point made, they were ordered to stop. Soon thereafter, Moscow formally recognized the separatist statelets of South Ossetia and Abkhazia, thus redrawing the post-Soviet borders for the first time. This was a loud warning shot. However, it was soon muted by the avalanche of the global financial crisis. A short-lived reset between Washington and Moscow followed.

In a somewhat similar move, reacting to the 2014 Maidan revolution in Kiev, which brought to power pro-Western elements within the Ukrainian elite in a coalition with western Ukrainian nationalists, Russian forces took control of Crimea (where Russia had long had a naval base), threatened to use military force elsewhere in Ukraine, staged a referendum in majority-Russian Crimea on joining Russia, formally incorporated the peninsula into the Russian Federation as a result, and actively supported an armed rebellion in Ukraine's southeastern Donbass region. This time, Russia not only redrew borders; it annexed territory, claiming the right to protect the interests of its co-ethnics. Many countries with Russian minorities became immediately concerned, from the Baltic States in NATO to Russia's own allies in the Collective Security Treaty Organization such as Belarus and Kazakhstan.

Restoration of military power

Moscow's more assertive foreign policy has been backed up by a reconstituted military force. After the 2008 Georgia war, Russian military reform began in earnest, and the decline of Russian military power which had lasted two decades began to be reversed. In 2010, a large-scale program of military modernization was adopted, with the stated aim of raising the share of "modern" weapons and equipment in the Russian arsenal from 30 to 70 percent by 2020. Military training and exercises were substantially upgraded. Russian military aircraft resumed routine patrols along the borders of the United States, the United Kingdom and other NATO countries, as well as Japan.

Even as Russia's power began to grow, Moscow refused to live by the constraints imposed on it in its hour of weakness. When NATO countries refused to ratify the adapted Conventional Forces in Europe (CFE) Treaty, raising objections of the Russian military presence in Georgia and Moldova, Russia suspended its implementation of the original 1990 CFE document, which was negotiated when the Warsaw Pact was still around and which limited Russian troop movements within its own territory. With neither the adapted nor the original CFE treaty in operation, the risks of a surprise attack in Europe have grown.

The actual employment of force in Crimea in 2014 and in Syria in 2015 returned Russia to the ranks of major conventional military powers. The Crimea operation featured a very different military than the one that saw battle in Georgia six years previously, not to speak of the decayed army that fought in Chechnya in the 1990s. The actual use of

Russian air and naval power in Syria was even more impressive. Russia's post-Cold War military weakness has become history. Countries with strained relations with Moscow had to take notice.

Yet this concern needs to be put in perspective. Russia's military power is a far cry from that of the United States. The Russian military budget is a small fraction of America's. It trails far behind China's. Except in the category of strategic and tactical nuclear weapons, there is no balance between Russia and the US, not to speak of a comparison with NATO. The new emerging front line in Europe passes just a hundred miles west of St Petersburg. Kaliningrad is completely surrounded on land by NATO territory. Similarly, the scale and intensity of Russia's military operations, from the Balkans to the Middle East, are dwarfed by those of the United States and its allies. And Russia has practically no allies.

Hybrid warfare

Many Russians have recently grown accustomed to quoting Emperor Alexander III, that Russia has only two friends in the world – its army and its navy. However, to protect and actively promote its interests, Russia is not relying solely on its military instruments. In the areas of conflict in the post-Soviet space, it has used a number of local allies – pro-Russian political formations, businesses and paramilitary groups – as well as bona fide volunteers and military advisers, specialists and other personnel from Russia. This heterogeneous combination of assets has made it possible to wage what has been called in the West "hybrid warfare" – in reality, the combined employment of military, paramilitary and non-military means in support of political objectives, which also made it more difficult to accuse Russia of direct military intervention.

The use of these assets in Crimea allowed Moscow to claim absolute victory "without firing a shot." In Donbass, the situation was less favorable to Russia, and Moscow's intervention carried a risk of escalation to an all-out war. However, the Kremlin managed to keep its direct military involvement on the ground to the minimum required to keep the cities of Donetsk and Lugansk off limits to Kiev's forces and to preserve the vital cross-border link between the rebel republics and the Russian Federation. Throughout the active phase of the conflict, Moscow carefully stuck to the position of "plausible deniability" with regard to its actual involvement. The Kremlin summarily dismissed

Western accusations of lying, basically assuming that, after the breach of trust between Russia and the West in Ukraine, few holds there were barred.

"Hybrid warfare," Crimea- or Donbass-style, however, can hardly be used where it is feared most: in the Baltic States and Poland. Moscow's intentions aside, the local Russians' self-identification with the Russian Federation cannot be compared to that of the Crimeans. Even though naturalization in Latvia and Estonia was made hard for local Russians, they are not looking to Moscow for protection and guidance. Daugavpils is not Donetsk-in-waiting, and Narva is no Lugansk. Poland is an even more far-fetched case. The Donbass model is not easily transferable, and employing it on the territory of a NATO member state denies the Kremlin any rationality whatsoever.

The energy weapon

The continuing steep rise in oil prices from 2000 to 2008 gave some Russians an idea that their resource-rich country could be an energy superpower, and its oil and particularly gas exports might be used as a tool of foreign policy – or, to put it simply, as an energy weapon. Rather maladroitly, Moscow used the threat of cutting off gas, which it sometimes executed, as a powerful argument in disputes with post-Soviet neighbors about energy price and other commercial issues. Not infrequently, these issues were richly mixed with politics, as in Ukraine after the Orange revolution in 2006 and 2009. In those disputes, the Western media and the public invariably sided with the victims of Gazprom's energy blockades. Even though Russia never stopped supplying its Western customers with gas – not even at the time of the Soviet Union's collapse – its reputation as a reliable supplier suffered.

As relations with Moscow began to sour in the mid-2000s, the West's dependence on Russian gas supplies – roughly 30 percent of the EU's imports – became a security concern, particularly in Poland, the Baltic States, Sweden, Britain and the United States. The fear here was that, by making Europe's countries, including the EU powerhouse Germany, dependent on Russian gas supplies, Moscow was achieving undue influence over their policies and left other countries such as Poland and the Baltic States exposed to Russian diktat. What the United States, Poland and the Baltics really feared, however, was a Russo-German economic symbiosis – which Putin was advocating – that would ultimately lead to Germany distancing itself from America, taking on a more independent international role, and becoming more "understanding" of Russia's geopolitical interests.

Particularly suspicious to the critics were direct Russian–German energy links, such as the North Stream gas pipeline across the Baltic Sea, which did not cross any third country territory, and thus, the fear ran, Gazprom held the countries in between – Poland and Lithuania – to ransom. A similar Gazprom plan to build a pipeline, dubbed the South Stream, to Italy and Austria across the Black Sea and the Western Balkans would have gone around Ukraine and left it in the lurch, making it a blind alley and also robbing cash-strapped Kiev of transit fees. The plan, moreover, might also have increased Russian influence in the Balkans and Southern Europe – Italy and Greece. The EU's opposition to the South Stream was strong enough to block it in 2014. Any future expansion of the North Stream, despite Berlin's clear interest in it, is meeting active resistance in Brussels, Warsaw and Washington.

With the end of the commodities super-cycle and the collapse of the oil price in 2014–16, the use of energy as an instrument of political pressure has become impractical. Moreover, the countries which feared such pressure – Poland, Lithuania, and now pro-Western Ukraine – have taken steps to minimize or even end their historic dependence on Russian direct energy supplies. In the case of Ukraine, this applies not only to purchases of Russian gas but also to electricity. As of 2016, Russia is delivering only coal to Kiev. The situation has reversed itself: the low oil price, which is hitting Russia very hard, has become a powerful factor in the Western strategy of "disciplining" Moscow. This invites a parallel to the mid-1980s, when the Saudi-engineered collapse of the oil price drove Gorbachev to the wall, turned the Soviet Union into a major debtor, and limited Moscow's freedom of maneuver.

Cyber capabilities

Russia has other means of impacting on other countries and influencing their behavior. It has a powerful cyber warfare capacity, which it probably used against Estonia in 2007, Georgia in 2008 and Ukraine in 2015. None of these cases, however, was decisive in the conflicts between Russia and the neighboring states. Georgia and Ukraine lost on the actual battlefield, not the virtual one, and Estonia did not change its policies on moving Soviet monuments and war graves away from Tallinn's city center. Moreover, Tallinn has since become a NATO center for countering cyber warfare operations.

In a cyber war, Russia would certainly be a formidable foe. Its capabilities in the field add to its nuclear arsenal as an effective deterrent to the United States. International agreements on cyber security, a twenty-first-century equivalent of twentieth-century nuclear arms control, are many years away. While the area remains much more impervious to outside observers than nuclear weapons and missile technology, there are good reasons to believe that the United States and its allies are at least as advanced there as are Russia and China. And they too use cyber weapons when they see a need for it – as against Iran.

Portraying the United States and NATO as a threat to Russia

When on New Year's Eve 2016 Russia adopted its new national security strategy, most Western commentators highlighted the portions of the document which referred to the United States and NATO actions as a threat to Russia. The document itself, however, hardly breaks new ground. Rather, it sums up the changes which have occurred since the beginning of the Ukraine crisis in 2014. Moscow does see the enhancement of NATO's military infrastructure in the Baltic States and Poland, the US and other foreign military deployments in Eastern Europe and the adjacent waters and airspace, and US missile defenses in Poland and Romania as posing a military threat to Russia, and it will respond in kind.

Many observers point out that Moscow's "declaration of a threat from the West" is largely beamed at the domestic audience. It may be annoying to many Europeans and Americans that the Kremlin is now using Russian–Western confrontation as a source of domestic support. In the recent era of Russian–Western cooperation, however, there were similar complaints in the United States and Europe that the Kremlin was using good relations with the West to legitimize its rule. That the Kremlin can thrive politically on both good and bad relations with the West says something about the Russian political system, Russian society and the Kremlin's ability to manage it, but hatred of the West is clearly not an obsession with the Russian leadership, which remains essentially pragmatic.

A bigger issue is Russia's self-isolation as a result of the deepening estrangement from the rest of Europe and the West. This is happening not only as a result of Russian-imposed counter-boycotts, such as the food embargo against the EU, and the multiplying elements of xenophobia in the public domain, but also on account of the new penury which makes Russians buy fewer foreign goods, cut back on foreign travel, and keep their children in the country. The notion of the West "ganging up" on Russia has undercut the empathy toward Europe which prevailed not only in the two decades after the end of the Cold War but had existed even in the Soviet period. The already wide gulf between Russia and Europe keeps growing.

Russian political threat to Europe

When Russia was rich, money was considered its prime political weapon. Moscow, it was often claimed, could exploit the interests of various business circles, above all in Europe, in the Russian market, to the Russians' advantage. Surprisingly for Moscow, these groups chose not to protest too loudly against the sanctions imposed on Russia in 2014 and have accepted significant losses as a result. However, they may not have given up entirely on the potential profits of Russian trade and economic cooperation. Some have left, while others have managed to adapt to the sanctions regime. Most are looking forward to the day when the sanctions are eased or lifted.

Sanctions, however, are not Russia's worst problem. After growth ground to a halt in 2013, Russia has been in a deep economic recession. When and if Russia comes up with a new economic model of development to replace the now inoperable one based on a high and rising price for oil, European and other Western investors will start paying attention again. This is likely to be a long wait, at best. Meantime, money, which used to be called Russia's main tool for getting ahead with "greedy Westerners," has become scarce. Like the energy weapon, the money weapon is now in other hands. It is the United States that decides how much of Russia it wants in the global money market.

Quite apart from the money magnet, there are also political groups within the European Union who occasionally side with Moscow on various issues. These range from the unease about US dominance (felt, e.g., within the German Die Linke party or among a few of France's surviving true Gaullists), to US spying on its allies (even among Chancellor Merkel's CDU associates), to anti-Brussels nationalism (as among Marine Le Pen's voters in France or Viktor Orbán's supporters in Hungary). Most of these forces are either left or right of center, which makes it difficult for Moscow to build ideological alliances with them. Some European nationalists, such as the Polish PiS party, are vehemently hostile to Moscow. The Kremlin's pragmatism is good for tactical connections but prevents long-term cooperation. As for the European political mainstream, it is largely skeptical or inimical to Russia's policies.

Even where there is a certain amount of popular support for friendly relations with Russia, the political elite remains largely Western-oriented. In Moldova, with its mercurial and notoriously corrupt politics, even the Communist Party headed by a former Russian police general is pro-EU. Serbia, for all its occasional Russophile rhetoric, is on track toward long-term integration into the European Union. Montenegro is soon to be admitted to NATO. Bulgarian elites are historically anti-Russian, having joined with Germany against Russia in both world wars. Greece, like Hungary, is using Russian connections as a bargaining chip in their relations with the EU. Cyprus used to profit hugely from Russian money on the island, but it obeyed the eurozone demands which hit Russian depositors very hard.

Russia is usually accused of implementing divide-and-rule policies toward the European Union. It is indeed difficult not to engage in this practice, given the absence of a common foreign policy in the EU. The twenty-eight member states of the EU have differing interests, experiences and views of Russia. There are the former Soviet republics Estonia, Latvia and Lithuania, annexed by the Soviet Union in 1940; there is Poland, divided several times by Russia and Germany; but there is also France, with strong historical and cultural ties; Austria, with strong business connections; and Germany, with its rich and twisted history of relations with Russia, which remarkably reached the point of historical reconciliation that permitted the country's reunification in 1990.

Any outside power – be that the United States or China – dealing with a Europe which is more than a common market but less than a federation would be seeking the best ways to promote its interests through individual influential members of the Union besides going to Brussels. Russia, with its centuries-long history of relations with all European countries, has been doing this naturally. To the Russians, Europe is still mainly Germany, France, Britain, Italy and Spain, plus two dozen middle- and small-sized countries. However, any advances that the Russians have been able to make in relations with one member can be checked and reversed by other members less friendly toward Moscow. With the accession of Central and Eastern European states to the EU, the skeptics have won a *de facto* veto on ties with Russia that are too close. After Berlin toughened its stance toward Moscow, the Union's most powerful country also joined the ranks of the skeptics. So much for the argument about Russian-fed Trojan horses inside the EU.

Shrinking spheres of influence

For all the talk of Russia's bullying its neighbors, which is not without foundation, what is most striking is how little influence Moscow actually wields beyond its borders, even in the former USSR. Russia's "sphere of influence" is actually limited to the territories it physically sustains and protects: Abkhazia; Donetsk and Lugansk; South Ossetia; and Transnistria. Even Moscow-allied Belarus often acts rather independently from Russia. Minsk still recognizes Georgia and Ukraine in their 1991 borders and keeps active relations with both Tbilisi and Kiev; it has become a prime re-exporter of the EU foodstuffs that Moscow banned from crossing into Russia, and President Alexander Lukashenko is adamant that Belarus remains a sovereign country, independent from Russia. Kazakhstan is even more explicit in following its "multi-vector" foreign policy. Its president, Nursultan Nazarbaev, was offended by Vladimir Putin's suggestions of Kazakhstan's statehood being only a "recent" phenomenon and was reportedly "unnerved" by the Russian Navy's October 2015 cruise missile strikes at Syria from the Caspian. The Moscow-led Collective Security Treaty Organization, which also includes Armenia, Kyrgyzstan and Tajikistan, is remarkable for the lack of solidarity among its members with its *de facto* leader, Russia.

In the quarter-century since the Soviet Union's disintegration, Russia has been dealing with the ruling elites in the newly independent states, usually seeking trade-offs with them, often subsidizing them, and – until very recently – ignoring their domestic opposition. For two decades it was prepared to stick to the 1991 borders and abandoned that stance only when the Kremlin saw a threat of NATO closing in, first in Georgia and then in Ukraine. So far, Russia has been reacting to revolutions and coups in the neighborhood rather than plotting and staging them. In Eastern Europe, Russia has finally "lost" Ukraine and Moldova; it has had to accept the massive growth of China's economic and political influence in Central Asia and that of America (in Georgia) and Turkey (in Azerbaijan) in the South Caucasus. In the future, Russia's sphere of influence is more likely to shrink further than to expand. The Russian Empire is definitely not making a comeback.

Use of ethnic Russians abroad as a destabilizing "fifth column"

For about a decade and a half after the break-up of the Soviet Union, defending the rights of compatriots abroad – i.e., some 25 million Russians who were left behind in the newly independent states when the Russian state receded to its current borders – was a fringe activity perpetrated by Russian nationalists, often in opposition to the Kremlin. It was only in 2008 that President Dmitri Medvedev, in the wake of the Georgia war, fought ostensibly to protect South Ossetians against Georgian "genocide" and declared Russia's right to defend and protect its co-ethnics, particularly in former Soviet territory, which was termed a "zone of privileged interests" of the Russian Federation.

In 2008, this essentially applied to the Ossetians, whom Georgian President Saakashvili tried to bring back, alongside their self-declared republic, into

Georgia. Six years later, this argument was used by President Putin to support the actions he had ordered in Crimea and with regard to Donbass. Putin talked about Russians as "the world's biggest divided nation," put forth the concept of Novorossiya ("New Russia," a historical term for the northern Black Sea coast conquered by Russia from the Ottoman Empire in the late eighteenth century) for the Russian-speaking southern and eastern provinces of Ukraine, and discussed "the Russian world" as a habitat of Russophones and those who associate themselves with Russian culture and the Russian state.

This provoked Putin's critics to draw comparisons with Hitler's policies of bringing all Germans under one roof and the use of German minorities to undermine neighboring countries before their annexation or subjugation. Not only Latvia and Estonia, with their proportionally large contingents of ethnic Russians, many of them still – twenty-five years after independence – without the citizenship of their countries of origin, but also Russia's own allies, such as Belarus and Kazakhstan, became worried. It took some time for the neighboring countries to see that the analogy with Hitler was wrong: the Kremlin had no plans to stoke ethnic tensions in order to destabilize and then annex former Soviet lands.

Agents of influence in the West

In the days of the abundance of financial resources, Russian money was considered to be a major tool in the hands of the Kremlin to buy influence in the West, not only "wholesale" but in a retail mode as well, recruiting "agents of influence." In the most celebrated case, Gerhard Schroeder, soon after resigning as German chancellor in 2005, agreed to serve as chairman of the board of North Stream, Gazprom's pipeline to Germany. A number of other senior Western businessmen, retired politicians and the like were offered positions in Russian companies, including some that were state-owned. Many accepted. A Washington K Street public relations company, Ketchum, was tasked with improving Russia's public image in the West.

Certainly, Russians then were looking for partners and image-makers in Europe and America to help them move around and integrate into the wider West which they aspired to join. They were doing what others – Asians, Middle Easterners, and the like – were doing before them. They were probably doing less than those others. And, clearly, Russian penetration of Western societies was no match for Western penetration of the Russian government in the early to mid-1990s, when US and

European advisers acted at times as decision-makers in Russian ministries. Yet, this is definitely passé. In the current climate in Europe and the United States, being linked to Russian interests is a kiss of death for anyone with a public career in mind. Russia is now more appealing to retired actors and sports figures.

Russian spying in the West was an issue during the Cold War. Then there was a brief period, in the early 1990s, when a premium was laid on cooperation on issues of common concern, such as non-proliferation, terrorism and transnational crime. In a sincere and unique but obviously foolish step, the Russians in 1991 even gave the Americans plans of their listening devices in the US embassy in Moscow. CIA officials, such as Robert Gates, were fêted in Moscow as colleagues and nearly comrades-in-arms. In 2001, Putin ordered the General Staff to give full intelligence support to the US operation in Afghanistan. The return of adversity in Russia–NATO relations saw, predictably, a fresh expansion of traditional and new (cyber, etc.) intelligence activities. Still, what struck the Europeans in recent years more than reports of Russian intelligence becoming more active were the revelations of friendly spying on them and their leaders by their senior ally, the United States.

Russian authoritarianism and kleptocracy

For the Western liberal establishment, the very nature of the Russian political and economic system is a threat. In the Western mind, Russia has long been associated with tsarist autocracy, then communist totalitarianism, and now authoritarian kleptocracy. Its successive political systems have been the very antithesis of the rule of law, political freedom and human rights. Now, it is clearly authoritarian, despite the formal trappings of democracy. Its political economy is bureaucratic capitalism, which lives off natural resources and favors those closest to the center of power. Property rights are conditional, and the legal system is managed by the powers that be. Civil society is under pressure.

The present primacy of the *raison d'état* – when corporate interests have been satisfied – rests on the memories, ideas and ideals taken from the past. Today's Russia is frankly statist, patriotic/ nationalistic and revisionist. Having lost the state in the botched attempt at reform under Gorbachev, the Kremlin is now focused on upholding its own supremacy. Having lost their empire, Russians are now in the process of building a multi-ethnic nation-state which puts a premium on nationalism. And, having been unable and unwilling to adapt to the US-dominated post-Cold War world, Russia is out to rebel against it, breaking the written and unwritten rules of behavior as it seeks to obtain recognition for its great-power status.

The Byzantine system of governance still prevailing in Russia makes the Kremlin decision-making process opaque, while the concentration and centralization of power in the hands of the sole individual at the top provides for policy steps which can be both sudden and surprising to outsiders. Whereas, in the US system, taking a decision on the use of force can take a lot of time and require a major effort at the inter-agency level, as well as between the White House and Congress, in the Russian system, one man essentially decides all. As a result, Russia can move very quickly, and by stealth, surprising even seasoned outside observers – as in Crimea, Donbass and Syria.

Russia: apart from Europe rather than a part of Europe

Many in the West traditionally view Russia as a country apart from Europe, the classical "Other." The 1990s Western debate on the "borders of Europe," which accompanied the NATO/

EU enlargement process, revealed strongly held convictions – though by no means universal – that Russia was, indeed, an outsider, which could at best be a partner of Europe, not part of it. In the late 2000s and 2010s, the center of gravity shifted to the view of Russia as an authoritarian alternative to the European values, norms and principles. Initially, the view of a "Russian model" was supported by the country's rapid oil-fired economic growth. When the growth stalled and was followed by recession, Russia came to be portrayed as a country that bullies its neighbors and corrupts everyone around.

Indeed, the Kremlin has a different approach than the EU governments to a number of important issues: state sovereignty, the use of military force, and the world order. Angela Merkel was right to say in 2014 that Vladimir Putin lives in a different world. This is a realist's world. Whereas the countries of Europe, and Germany above all, have largely transcended their troubled history, Russia is still going through it. But, truth be told, wherever Russia may be, it keeps company there with much of the rest of the world. The EU is a happy exception: not even the United States, with its distinct view of America's exceptionalism, sovereignty, military power and world order – one "American century" succeeding another – is where Europe is on these issues.

To strengthen the case of Russia's un-European nature, adherents of that view pointed to official Russian concepts of the country as a separate Eurasian civilization, facing both the East and the West. These concepts, of course, have deep roots in Russian history – and this is another issue of concern to the West.

Treatment of history

Post-Soviet Russia's unwillingness to do to the Soviet Union's legacy what West Germans had done to that of the Third Reich is disturbing to quite a few people in Europe. In Russia, the Communist Party was not put on trial, nor were its members limited in their political rights. The Soviet Union itself is viewed as a historical form of the Russian state, a seventy-year period in Russia's millennium of history, a legitimate polity rather than a criminal aberration – even though officially the Romanov dynasty is revered and the Bolshevik revolution is rejected. In this scheme of things, Stalin, the World War II commander-in-chief and builder of the Soviet state, is a more respectable figure, despite his well-known crimes, than Lenin, who destroyed the Russian imperial state and worked for Russia's defeat in World War I.

This reading of history jars with the views of those in Eastern and Central Europe who see their countries primarily as victims of both the Soviet Union and, before it, the Russian Empire. What is most sacred in the Russian history textbook – the Soviet victory in World War II – appears to many in Europe's east as a replacement of Nazi rule by Soviet totalitarianism. In Estonia and Latvia, those who served with the Wehrmacht and even the German SS between 1941 and 1945 are recognized as national heroes, while those who fought on the side of the Red Army are termed occupiers. Present-day Ukraine puts Soviet World War II veterans and the nationalists who fought against them, also in alliance with the Nazis, on an equal footing. While Russia and Poland made a productive effort in the late 2000s and the early 2010s to discuss the dark issues of their common history, there is unlikely to be much agreement between the Russians, on the one hand, and the Baltic countries, on the other.

In the victims' optic, Russia is equated with communism and its most brutal practices. The famine which in 1932–3 hit large parts of the Soviet Union, including Ukraine, southern and central Russia, and

Kazakhstan, is officially characterized by Kiev as genocide of the Ukrainian people by Moscow. The fact that Stalin, six decades after his death, is still viewed by a large portion of the Russian population as a great leader is presented as testimony to the evergreen penchant of the Russian people for a strong hand, even an exceedingly cruel one. That, for a lot of ordinary Russian people today Stalin is, however unlikely, a protest symbol against rampant corruption, is usually overlooked.

* * *

The fears described above are based on facts and have long roots in history. Russia is authoritarian and has a distinct view of itself as a great power. To the Europeans, Russia, a near neighbor sharing the continent with them but politically and ideologically alien, denies them the promise of a "Europe whole and free," a "*europäische Friedensordnung.*" It also evokes the bitter memories of the past century and suggests frightening parallels.

These memories and parallels, however, paint a picture which does not exist now and has no chance of emerging in the future. Russia has no resources and no real will to re-create its Eurasian empire, all the more so because the would-be parts of that empire would resist being included in it;

it has no ambition to conquer neighboring EU/NATO member states, thus risking a war with the US; its brand of authoritarianism is a domestic, not an export product; its state-dominated economic system is not a model for others to emulate; its ideology is nationalistic, not international; and its capacity to infiltrate Western societies is very modest.

If anything, the West should fear Russia's weakness more than its strength. A quarter-century after the Soviet implosion, the country is very brittle. It is now going through a major economic crisis, which has structural roots; the modicum of political stability which exists depends essentially on the popularity of Vladimir Putin, thus hanging by a thread; and the absence of durable institutions within the present system and of a credible alternative to the current regime suggest that a serious political crisis, when it happens, might lead to chaos. Russia also gives precious little advance warning before it stirs; and, after it begins to stir, it soon starts to shake.

There is little that the outside world can do to affect the Russian internal political dynamic; the West needs, however, to see clearly the real challenge which Russia poses and find a constructive way of dealing with it.

2

The Russia Challenge

US Secretary of Defense Ashton Carter has put Russia at the top of the list of security challenges and threats to the United States, ahead of China, Iran, North Korea and ISIL.[10] So, what is Russia's challenge to the West?

What does Russia want?

Vladimir Putin's long leadership is essentially about two things: first, to keep Russia in one piece and, second, to return it to the ranks of the world's great powers. By the mid-2010s the first mission looked accomplished, with the country not merely united under the imperial presidency but with the president's personal popularity – or public acquiescence in him – standing at well above 80 percent. As for the second, in the Ukraine conflict Russia shook off the constraints imposed on it by the post-Cold War system; and, through its direct military intervention and parallel diplomatic activity in Syria, Russia has suddenly become indispensable in the issues of war and peace in one of the world's most turbulent regions – the Middle East. If there is a strategy behind the Kremlin's actions, here is its main objective.

In the past decade and a half, Russia's self-image has changed considerably. Putin and his entourage still view the country as European in origin, a successor to the Eastern Christian Byzantine tradition, but they see it primarily as fully sovereign – on a par with the rest of Europe, rather than an associate of the EU. A continent-size country, uniting Slavic, Turkic and scores of other ethnic elements, a home to four religions legally deemed indigenous – Orthodox Christianity, Islam, Judaism and Buddhism – Russia appears to these individuals a distinct geopolitical, economic and cultural unit, a potential center of attraction for neighbors in Eurasia, and a partner to those in the non-West advocating a multipolar world order.

In geopolitical and geostrategic terms, the Kremlin posits Russia as a great power with a global reach. It rejects as ludicrous or malicious any attempts to put Russia into a category of regional powers. Geography is the Kremlin's major asset: a country which borders directly on Norway and North Korea – as well as on America, China and Japan – and whose reach extends from the icy Arctic to the approaches to the Middle East and Afghanistan, cannot easily be boxed in. Russia's modest economic and demographic weight, the Kremlin argues, does not tell the whole story: the country has immense potential for growth and its demographics are improving. What is more important is the fact that Russia, alongside the United States and China, is at the moment one of the world's only three major independent military powers.

Russian official views on the global order traditionally favor great-power concert as the best means of managing the international system. Russia's Alexander I was one of the key players at the Vienna Congress of 1815, which ushered in the Concert of Europe and the Holy Alliance; thereafter, he and his successor Nicholas I were the dominant figures in Central and Eastern Europe. Joseph Stalin, in the company of US presidents and UK prime ministers at Tehran, Yalta and Potsdam in 1943–5, laid the foundation of the post-World War II global order, which divided Europe and the world. On the other hand, Mikhail Gorbachev tried but utterly failed to keep the Soviet Union intact and in play as a power center in the post-Cold War world, and Boris Yeltsin nearly accepted US leadership. Hence, Putin's mission to restore Russia's rightful place on the global scene.

Such elevation, however, cannot be achieved with the post-Cold War global order intact. The place Russia is seeking is that of a co-decision-maker, a country that co-writes the rules, watches over their application, and implements sanctions as necessary. Moscow's ideal is the pentarchy of the United Nations Security Council as a global concert, with Russia as its permanent, veto-wielding member. In fact, the implications of Russia's international "restoration" include checking US supremacy by subjecting the US itself to the authority of the UNSC. Russians can accept US pre-eminence, but not dominance.

Russia's ambitions, however, are not always backed up by the realities of power. Throughout its history, it has had to press hard, and often fight, in order to be recognized. It has learned to compensate for its deficiencies in military power, economic development and cultural standard. To succeed, it relied on quantity to offset quality, resorted to centralization and mobilization, displayed the temerity of punching way above its weight, demonstrated boldness and swiftness of action, and leaned on its time-tested capacity to pay a very high price to achieve its important goals.

After a period of good luck at the beginning of the twenty-first century in the form of ever rising oil prices, Russia was hit by their collapse, compounded by the structural problems of its own economy, the corrupt and stifling politico-economic system, and, on top of it all, the sanctions imposed upon Russia as a result of the Ukraine crisis. These are all massive challenges which put in question the capacity of the current ruling elite to hold the country together and lead it onto a path of economic development. A failure to respond adequately to those challenges will have dire consequences for the sustainability of the entire system and the stability of the country itself.

Challenges to the United States

It is truly an irony of history that the United States should be overtly challenged by a party such as today's Russia – a country whose GDP is a small fraction of America's, whose share in the global trade is a mere 1 percent, and even whose defense budget is a tenth of the Pentagon's.

To most educated Americans, Russia is the day before yesterday's news, a country on the long and irreversible trajectory of decline. It is a third- or fourth-tier actor in a remote corner of the globe, with a contemptible leadership mired in corruption, which can be a nuisance at best.

Figures of comparison, however, do not tell the whole story. Among the countries of the world, Russia has a unique quality: its ruling elite and its people strongly reject domination of the international system by any one power. And Russians are ready to push back when they see their own interests in danger, despite the long odds. Unlike the Chinese, the Russians are anything but incremental in their approach to world hegemons: they are bona fide in-your-face people.

In 2014, the Russians may have jumped the gun, and faced the consequences, but Russia's rebellion against the post-Cold War order does not run against the current global trend. If anything, the Russians have found themselves ahead of the curve, but not too much. The quarter-century period of amicable relations among all the major powers, guaranteed by US near-hegemony in the system, a sort of Pax Americana, is over. China and India, Iran and Saudi Arabia, are becoming increasingly active in their respective neighborhoods. Major power relations are again becoming an issue, and their movements will reshape the global order.

Eastern Europe

In Eastern Europe, the United States has had to live since 2014 with a status quo which it does not accept. Washington has failed to make its rules stick and walked back from the assurances of Ukraine's territorial integrity contained in the 1994 Budapest memorandum, which the United States signed alongside Britain and Russia. Few people in the world believe that Russia will hand Crimea back to Ukraine. Donbass remains an issue, where Moscow keeps insisting on a compromise political solution which Kiev resists. The result is another frozen conflict. The United States has no leverage to make Russia back down under pressure. Even though overall US power clearly dwarfs that of Russia, the stakes for Moscow in Ukraine are so much higher than Washington's, and the Kremlin is prepared to go to much greater lengths. If push comes to shove, Americans would hardly send their sons and daughters to defend Ukraine. As a result, the "balance of will" in the former Soviet Union is not in America's favor.

In response to the Russian challenge, the United States has been able to consolidate allies and reinvent NATO for the mission for which it had been originally designed. However, what one is witnessing is not exactly the Cold War revisited. Most Americans do not see Russia as a threat. Thus, a new commitment to the defense of Europe is, to many, an unnecessary distraction from more important issues, such as the fight against ISIL. Sensing this, America's new allies in Eastern and Central Europe fear that the United States will leave them in the lurch and deal with Russia behind their backs. The Baltic States and even Poland are worried that Russia will attack and occupy them, with the United States unable to protect their allies and unwilling to risk a nuclear exchange with Russia for the sake of Eastern Europeans.

As a result, the demand for a US presence on the ground in Europe's east will be greater, but so will be the risks for the United States itself, in a situation which few Americans will find existential. The downing by Turkey, a NATO member, of a Russian warplane in Syria in 2015 is a case in point. An incident like this could have been much more dangerous over the Baltic or the Black Sea. For the time being, the United States has decided to rotate a brigade-size force in Eastern Europe to create a quasi-permanent military presence in the area, but this may anger the Russians more than reassure the Balts and the Poles.

The Middle East

In the Middle East, Russia reinserted itself into the region dominated for a quarter-century solely by the US. In doing this, Moscow broke the informal American monopoly on the legitimate use of force – and, so far, has got away with it. At minimum, Russia's intervention carried the risk of inadvertent collision between US and Russian aircraft, but it also opened the possibility in Syria of a US–Russian war by proxy. Even when those risks were initially managed, Russia's proactive diplomacy exploited the effect of its military engagement and returned Moscow as a player in the Middle East, hardly a welcome development for the United States. As already noted, this brought the Kremlin closer to its goal of reclaiming great-power status beyond the former Soviet space.

As the United States chose to work with Russia to produce a political settlement in Syria, it effectively played along with Moscow's ambitions. Ever since John Kerry's first visit as secretary of state to the Kremlin in May 2013, Vladimir Putin was suggesting something like a Dayton-à-deux solution in Syria, with Moscow and Washington as its two co-sponsors. At that point, this was unacceptable to the United States. Putin, however, deftly used Barack Obama's reluctance to bomb Damascus after the chemical attack to offer a plan of Syria's chemical disarmament as an alternative to US military strikes. Despite many doubts, the plan worked, with the US and Russia leading an international effort that, amid the civil war there, rid Syria of chemical weapons.

In 2015, the Russian military intervention, coupled with Europe's influx of a million migrants, many from Syria, pushed the United States to probe the Russian Dayton formula. The Vienna/Geneva process has been exceedingly difficult, partly because even a US–Russian accord does not guarantee success without the endorsement of regional players, above all Iran and Saudi Arabia. Yet, even without the agreement, the very image of Russia and the United States presiding over the newest peace process in the Middle East helps to confer on Russia the status it covets. Such duopoly creates uncertainty among some of Washington's allies and partners that the US is dealing with Russia over their heads.

Greater Eurasia

While the "little Eurasia" of the former Soviet republics is unlikely to coalesce in the form of a new USSR or the historical Russian Empire, a Greater Eurasia is emerging, driven by China's march westward and Russia's coincidental turn to the east.

Gone are the days at the turn of the century when the United States could claim to be the dominant power in Eurasia. For the first time since the empire of Genghis Khan, the great continent of Eurasia – from the Western Pacific to the Eastern Atlantic – is being integrated thanks to the dynamics coming primarily from Asia. This has the potential of changing all of Eurasia beyond recognition.

The Russian–Chinese rapprochement and Beijing's and Moscow's reciprocal westward and eastward turns predate the Ukraine crisis, but both were given a boost by the breakdown of Russia's relations with the West. True, there has been and will be no "geopolitical merger" as a result. An alliance between China and Russia looks unlikely, but the present bilateral relationship is much more than the "strategic partnership" it is formally dubbed. It is certainly more than a marriage of convenience. For lack of a better word, the state of relations can be described as an *entente*. This denotes a degree of mutual empathy and geopolitical convergence based on overlapping worldviews and a joint resentment of US global dominance.

Most Americans are relaxed about the prospects of China and Russia drawing closer together. Any alliance between Beijing and Moscow, their logic goes, would have China on top. Russia, however, will not enjoy being a junior partner to China and will seek to break away from its tight embrace. In such a scenario, only one credible option will remain open to Moscow: seek reconciliation with Washington and some form of association with the European Union. This would mean Russia's geopolitical surrender.

This reasoning is not flawless. The situation in Eurasia can change to the disadvantage of the United States. For all their reported contempt for the Russians, the Chinese have been very considerate and careful when dealing with their northern neighbors. Since the normalization of their relations with Moscow in 1989, they have been able to achieve so much more with Russia than the West, while evoking practically no pushback from the Russians. The Chinese appreciate the value of appearances and do not humiliate the Russians publicly, whatever they might think of them in private. Beijing's centralized control not only over policy but also over public discussion of policy protects the relationship from unnecessary provocations.

Each country is wary of coming too close to the other. China and Russia, however, can continue to consolidate and upgrade their relationship short of an alliance. In this case, more of Russia's natural and military-technological resources would be made available to China. Strategic coordination between

Moscow and Beijing would remain loose, but, in the larger scheme of things concerning the world order, Beijing and Moscow will be on the same side. The Greater Eurasia that they are constructing will not be run from a single center, but their continental entente will essentially be aimed at limiting US dominance on the edges of the continent and in the world at large.

Strategic stability and arms issues

Despite the Pentagon's towering position in the global military field, the latter offers some advantages to Moscow. Russia remains a nuclear superpower, in an exclusive league with the United States. The nuclear deterrent is back in play in US–Russian relations, countering President Obama's grand vision of a world less reliant on nuclear weapons. While nuclear is back, arms control is frozen and may even be on the way out. There is virtually no prospect in the foreseeable future of new US–Russian strategic arms reduction agreements. The advent of strategic non-nuclear systems and strategic defenses complicates the task of any future negotiators. The arrival of China as a major military power makes bilateral US–Russian arms control increasingly insufficient and obsolete, while any trilateral deals are technically exceedingly complex and, for the time being, politically impossible.

The Russia Challenge

Outside of the nuclear field, Russia's military, of course, is not the Pentagon's peer. Yet, it is re-emerging as a capable force which can make a difference in a number of theaters, from the Middle East to Central Asia to the Arctic. With post-Cold War security arrangements in Europe now history, there are dangers of uncontrolled military activity along the new line of Russia–NATO confrontation in Eastern Europe. Incidents in the air and at sea, provocative war games scenarios, and troops and weapons deployments create a vast potential for miscalculation in an area which has been considered safe for twenty-five years.

Russia remains a top global exporter of arms and military technology, second only to the United States. Even in the times of current crisis, the defense industry is prioritized by the Kremlin: the requirements of confrontation are compelling, plus it is being viewed as a locomotive for Russia's new industrialization. Russian arms deliveries to various countries, such as China, India or Iran, can and do affect local and regional balances. Russia is also well equipped in cyber warfare capabilities. These assets carry a major potential risk to the United States. At the other end of the spectrum, Russia has shown a capacity for waging "hybrid warfare," operating just under the threshold of conventional military operations.

Geo-economics

Russia has been the largest economy put under sanctions in recent times. In geo-economic terms, the US-orchestrated sanctions against Russia have exacerbated the process of global economic fragmentation. Russia has responded to the Western restrictions by imposing a food imports ban on the sanctioning countries, primarily members of the European Union. Traditionally strong economic relations between Russia and Ukraine have been broken. Following the spat with Ankara, Moscow initiated sanctions of its own against Turkey, until recently a major economic partner. Other countries, such as China, watching the Russian–Western economic wars are making conclusions for themselves about the ability of economic ties to provide stability to political relations. The global economic system that had been experiencing increasing strain for some time thus received a powerful blow.

Challenges to the European Union

The European Union was directly challenged by Moscow's response to its support for Ukraine's pro-Western orientation. The EU failed to appreciate the geopolitical, economic and even psychological importance of Ukraine to the Russian leadership and people and pursued its Eastern Partnership project without much thinking about its wider implications. At the crucial moment, as Ukraine's fate was being decided, European diplomacy failed to manage a soft landing for the Yanukovych regime and the ensuing power transfer, and thus the EU was exposed as an irrelevant and – in the Kremlin's view – an untrustworthy actor.

The Ukraine crisis that soon followed brought home to the European leaders, starting with Angela Merkel, both the harsh reality of war on the EU's very doorstep and the possibility of an even wider conflagration affecting members of the Union itself. This caught the EU off guard: it had not been equipped to deal with geopolitical crises. This was the responsibility of NATO – i.e., the US. On the other hand, bailing out Ukraine and helping it reform itself is a mighty challenge – one which falls mainly on the European Union.

Russia meanwhile has become even more divisive for the unity of the EU and for transatlantic relations. In the wake of the downing of the Malaysian airliner over Donbass in 2014, German and other European business circles, which had traditionally seen Russia as a major opportunity, acquiesced in their governments putting politics – or, some would say, principles – before profits. At the time, this was a remarkable achievement by Europe's politicians, given the volume of trade between the EU and Russia – about €1 billion a day in 2013. Since then, the volume of trade has halved.

However, this common stance on Russia is difficult to sustain over the long term. Different European countries have very different experiences with Russia, and very different expectations. Whereas the Baltic States and Poland are deeply worried about their former hegemon, and Sweden and Britain remain traditionally skeptical of the historical rival, France, Germany, Italy and Austria do not feel threatened and want to continue trading with Russia without constraints, while Greece and Cyprus are basically friendly. There is potential for individual countries opting out of the sanctions regime which, given the EU requirement of unanimity of decision-making on the issue, would terminate it.

So far, the Europeans have managed to stick together on Russia sanctions and to form a common front with the United States. It has been one of the major foreign policy accomplishments of the Obama administration that EU and US sanctions are essentially identical and offer no daylight to the Kremlin. Given the very light US exposure – in contrast to that of Europe – to Russian trade, US sanctions are expected to stay indefinitely, as there is no domestic constituency for removing them. If, however, the price of the EU keeping its sanctions on Russia becomes too great at some point, this would open a gap between Europeans and Americans that Moscow would welcome.

It is not only material issues that present the Europeans with challenges related to Russia. The Kremlin has adopted an ideology of conservatism or traditionalism and designated liberalism as an opponent. This, of course, does not prevent Moscow from being opportunistic when circumstances allow or demand it. Russian conservatism on such issues as the value of national sovereignty, the role of religion in society, or the importance and nature of the family, however, finds an echo in those quarters across Europe which are disillusioned with globalization and the European project. A more successful Russia and smarter Russian policy could in the future capitalize more in these areas.

Until the Ukraine crisis, Russia was pushing for some form of Euro-Russian confederacy, under the rubric of a "Greater Europe," from Lisbon to Vladivostok. This would have been based on a marriage between Russian resources and European industry, cemented by asset swaps, cross-investments and technology transfers, and various sorts of exchanges among people. Such a Europe would certainly have been whole, and might even – depending on the level of EU–Russian policy coordination – have played a global role, but at the price of distancing itself from the United States. Many Europeans with strong Atlanticist convictions were wary of the idea, which would have not so much tied Russia to the EU as the other way around. When Vladimir Putin laid out his plans to the German political and business communities in 2010, he got a cool reception from Angela Merkel.

Meanwhile, the challenge of Russia as "Greater Europe's" potentially dominant power has been succeeded by a different kind of challenge. Russia's alienation from Europe has coincided with its turn to the east, all the way to the Pacific. In 2012, the Customs Union of Belarus, Kazakhstan and Russia was upgraded to become a Eurasian Economic Union. The "Greater Europe" concept was thus transformed into a binary construct composed of the EU and the EEU. In 2015, Moscow agreed to "harmonize" the EEU with Beijing's "One Belt, One Road" initiative. The result could be a "Greater Eurasia" from Shanghai to St Petersburg. Long the east of the West, Russia could turn into the west of the East.

The ultimate challenge for the Europeans, of course, would be a Russia that breaks down and threatens to disintegrate. Should this happen – and this cannot be completely ruled out – it would create a major source of instability on Europe's eastern fringes. The much referred to "collapse" of the Soviet Union was in fact a more or less orderly dismantlement of its huge edifice. Of all exits from an empire, Russia's in the 1990s was one of the least bloody and most cheerful: Moscow itself was leading the process. There is no certainty, however, that a new "geopolitical catastrophe," should it occur, would be as mild. With all these issues at the back of one's mind, how has the West dealt recently with the Russian challenge?

3

Bringing Russia into Line

For a number of years, the Russian challenge, in gestation, was largely ignored. Russia was expected by some to bite the bullet and adapt or adjust to the new world-order realities. Others expected it to transform itself – e.g., from Saul to Paul. In any event, Russia was perceived as too weak to matter much; as sufficiently integrated into the global economy, on the one hand, and highly vulnerable because of its dependence on the oil price, on the other; and too corrupt to take on the West, for fear of having their hidden riches or dubious transactions exposed and risking court proceedings and even arrests. Essentially, this condition was expected to last a very long while.

The West as a whole did not have a Russia strategy: Russia simply was not an issue big enough to warrant that. The European Union, which on account of its geographical proximity had to pay more attention to Russia than the United States, became progressively disillusioned with the prospect of Russia's "Europeanization." The EU, however, does not operate as a strategic unit at all. As mentioned, the operators of the Eastern Partnership project grossly misjudged the stakes involved in Ukraine. When the Ukraine crisis broke out, the EU essentially withdrew to the background.

The United States has learned to look down on Russia, which was neither an issue nor a big enough partner. In Ukraine, the US, which had remained in the background during the Maidan stand-off, had to step forward when the Europeans proved unable to manage the crisis they had helped create. Washington soon forged a new NATO-wide approach to Russia which combined political isolation, economic pressure and information warfare, plus strengthening NATO and support for Ukraine itself. The policy's stated objective was to make the Kremlin back off on Ukraine and step back in line. Europe basically went along with it.

Political isolation

The Ukraine crisis first resulted in largely symbolic measures. Russia was *de facto* expelled from the

G8, which reverted to its more homogeneous G7 format. Cooperation in a number of other fora, from the NATO–Russia Council to the Parliamentary Assembly of the Council of Europe, was restricted or frozen. Top-level meetings and high-level contacts were reduced to the bare minimum. The aim was to demonstrate the West's strong disapproval of Moscow's policies and to send the message that there will not be business as usual until Moscow changes its behavior.

The result, after more than two years, has been the sealing of the chasm between the West and Russia. The relationship has taken a new, clearly adversarial quality. Mutual adversity is now the new normal. Political isolation, however, is little more than a phrase. There is nothing like an iron curtain physically separating Russia from the West, the way it was with the Soviet Union. Top-level visits became rare, but since the start of the Ukraine crisis President Putin has been to Austria, Australia, France, Hungary, Italy, Turkey and the United States, sometimes for multilateral summits. He has also toured key non-Western countries – Argentina, Brazil, China, India, Iran, and others – and received leaders of dozens of countries in Russia.

Other forms of communication were not broken off. Leaders' phone calls, particularly between Putin and Obama, and between Putin and Merkel, have become, if anything, more frequent. In 2015 alone, the US secretary of state and the Russian foreign minister met about twenty times. The Normandy format brought together the Russian president and the leaders of Germany and France, as well as Ukraine, to discuss the Ukraine crisis. Despite his supposed "isolation," Vladimir Putin held a number of informal but substantive meetings with Barack Obama.

True, there is no more warmth in these contacts, but they focus on issues that cannot be resolved without Russia – Ukraine, Iran and other non-proliferation concerns, and Syria. Russia, of course, remains a very active permanent member of the UN Security Council. It is also a member of the G20, and attempts to suspend it from the group were immediately rebuffed by China and other non-Western states. Against the background of deteriorating relations with the US and the EU, Russia's ties with non-Western countries – including in such clubs as BRICS and the Shanghai Cooperation Organization (SCO), whose back-to-back summits Putin hosted in 2015 – have grown, even though they do not replace or compensate for the broken ties with the West. Russia, no longer an aspiring candidate for membership in an expanded West, is now positioning itself as part of the global non-West.

Within Russia, alienation from the West has had the effect of rallying the bulk of the population around the flag, the Kremlin and Putin. The Western insistence that isolationist measures are directed against Putin's policies rather than the Russian people is not cutting much ice. Most Russians see Western attempts at isolating the Kremlin as a proof of the United States and its allies being Russia's historical competitors, and the Kremlin, to them, becomes a symbol of national resistance. True, this image, spread by state-controlled television, is not shared by the 20 percent or so who remain committed to Russia's European/Western vocation, but it rings many bells with the rest of the population. For the Kremlin, history is a very powerful ally. It is also joined by another highly improbably ally, economics.

Economic sanctions

Western disapproval of Russian policies in Ukraine did not remain symbolic for long. In July 2014 real punitive measures came. The aim of the "sectoral" sanctions, covering banking, high technology and other sectors of the economy, was to put pressure on members of Putin's inner circle, who were known to have substantial assets in the West; pinch hard the oligarchs who were used to borrowing in the West to keep their empires going; target several branches of the Russian economy as a whole, particularly the defense industry and oil exploration, by denying high-technology transfers to them; place Crimea off limits to international business; and, eventually, bring home to ordinary Russians that the Kremlin policies which they supported *en masse* carried a cost that they now had to bear.

The immediate result of these steps was manifold. The inner circle clung even closer to Putin: the sanctions have become a loyalty test, which they were all determined to pass. They were duly rewarded for their losses by new opportunities in Russia. For some, Western censure came as a badge of distinction which protected them from the president's displeasure on other grounds. The oligarchs faced a choice between staying in Russia and moving out. Some chose the latter, but most stayed: rather than being the real owners of their holdings, they were actually managing them on the Kremlin's behalf. The economy was offered the option of import substitution, including as a result of Russia banning food supplies from the sanctioning countries, and Crimea received an influx of federal transfers. As for the ordinary Sergeis and Natalias, they suddenly discovered that they were Russians.

Western sanctions, of course, had a major impact on the Russian economy. They added to the structural economic crisis that the country had entered in 2013. Stagnation turned into recession in the fall of 2014 as a result of the sharp drop in the price of oil, which continued to slide downward in 2015 and 2016. The lack of Western investment and technology transfers and the inability to raise finance in Western money markets are not the most serious elements of the current Russian economic recession, but they add to the severity of the crisis. This economic crunch remains the main hope of Western governments: that the Kremlin runs out of reserves to keep the country running and to maintain even the minimum support of the population, and so will have to start rolling back its policies.

This outcome will become evident only in several years' time: for the present moment, Moscow has enough resources to stay the course, even if some expenses have been trimmed or pushed back. The crisis is forcing the Kremlin toward hard choices in its economic policy, essentially between a more liberal approach to unchain the energies of the national business community, on the one hand, and an effort to mobilize all available resources under strict government control, on the other. Neither option, however, promises a softening of

Moscow's policies toward the West: a replay of the 1980s situation which thrust Mikhail Gorbachev into the hands of the Soviet Union's Western creditors, and constrained Moscow to make geopolitical concessions, is unlikely this time around. 2015 was a difficult year for the Russian companies which have had to repay Western loans, but as a result the country's corporate debt has markedly decreased.

While they are not part of a formal response to Russian actions in Ukraine, the European Union's steps to reduce dependence on Russian energy supplies have resulted in the forced abandonment of Gazprom's South Stream project which would have supplied gas to Southern and South-Eastern Europe. An expansion of Gazprom's other project, the North Stream, which connects Russia and Germany across the Baltic Sea, which Germany wants, is under pressure within the EU and from across the Atlantic. In conjunction with other measures, Gazprom's share of the EU's gas market has shrunk considerably. The energy relationship, the mainstay of EU–Russian trade, has frayed.

Support for eastern NATO countries

Next to putting pressure on Russia, supporting NATO allies on its borders has been a priority for Western leaders. In the wake of the Ukraine crisis, the three Baltic States – Estonia, Latvia and Lithuania – felt they might be the next targets of "Russian aggression" – a striking expression of their lack of confidence in the alliance which they had joined a decade before. Poland also felt exposed. NATO, at its September 2014 summit in Wales, essentially reclassified Russia as a problem rather than a partner and decided to build a rapid reaction force to deal with contingencies along its eastern frontier and to enhance the heretofore very light alliance presence in the eastern member states. Following that, some US heavy weapons were positioned in those countries, and NATO exercises were held there, sometimes virtually right across the border from Russia. As a next step, the United States will keep a rotating – and thus quasi-permanent – troop presence in the eastern NATO countries.

There is no evidence to suggest that Russia harbored any designs on the former Baltic republics of the Soviet Union, not to mention the former Soviet satellite Poland. NATO steps, however, are designed to provide a degree of reassurance to the eastern allies that they will not be left one-on-one with Russia in the event of a crisis. This is reminiscent of the Cold War situation, when US boots on the ground, rather than a formal pledge under Article 5 of the Washington Treaty, were considered a credible guarantee – a "tripwire" – of defense in the hour of need. Even that, however, was not enough then: remember the never-to-be-answered question of whether the United States would risk losing Chicago to defend Hamburg or West Berlin.

At the same time, expansion of NATO military infrastructure, not just the alliance's "political" membership, toward the Russian border is leading to consolidation of a new permanent stand-off between NATO and Russia. The "Suwalki gap" – 70 kilometers or so of Polish and Lithuanian territory which separate Kaliningrad from Belarus which, if controlled by Russian forces, could cut off the Baltics from mainland NATO territory – is taking the place in NATO's strategic minds of the famous Fulda gap on the former inner-German border. Add US missile defenses in Poland and Romania, and US Navy ships patrolling the Baltic and the Black Sea, and the message to Russia cannot be ignored.

The message, however, is inevitably read in Moscow not so much as a warning to keep off NATO territory as the United States and its allies demonstrating their capacity to apply military pressure on Russia, now from very close range. The Russian General Staff, which before the Ukraine crisis had regarded Russia's western border as relatively safe, is consequently revising the armed forces' posture, deployment pattern and military exercise scenarios. Kaliningrad, after all, is much bigger than West Berlin, and there are no constraints regarding the deployment there of powerful Russian weapons systems, including missiles. This, in turn, would only make the Baltic countries and Poland more nervous.

Supporting Ukraine and other non-NATO states

In 2014, Western countries gave immediate and full support to the leaders of the Euromaidan revolution that toppled the corrupt Yanukovych regime. Western support, however, was powerless to prevent the seizure of Crimea by Russian forces or the Russian intervention in Donbass. What NATO would have done in the event of a large-scale Russian invasion of Ukraine, which might have been an option considered by the Kremlin in 2014, is a moot point. In actual fact, the United States and its allies supplied Ukraine with intelligence and non-lethal military equipment, but stopped short of sending weapons which could have led to an escalation toward direct collision with Russia.

For the same reason, NATO membership for Ukraine is difficult to imagine while the conflict with Russia continues. Analogies with post-World War II Germany are far-fetched here, and, while they recognize Crimea as part of Ukraine, Western governments would not risk going to war with Russia over it. The United States, focused elsewhere, has *de facto* subcontracted daily management of the Ukraine crisis to Germany, flanked by France. The Minsk I and II agreements, which Berlin and Paris helped forge, resulted in a ceasefire in Donbass by the spring of 2015 and offered a tentative path to a political solution, but in reality they froze the conflict.

The terms of Minsk II, incidentally, are actually quite acceptable to Moscow but are anathema to Kiev. The agreement would result in Ukraine giving its regions, including Donbass, the power of veto over accession bids to alliances such as NATO and, moreover, would legitimize the anti-Maidan authorities in Donbass. No wonder that Kiev's best option is to sabotage the accord's implementation.

Ukraine's association with the European Union – the issue which sparked off the revolution in Kiev –

has been a reality since 2015. A deep free trade area between the EU and Ukraine is a fact, even if EU membership for the latter is at best a long way off. Trade between Ukraine and Russia has collapsed. Ukrainians are on track to visa-free entry into the Schengen countries, while Kiev has banned all air travel with Russia. Post-Maidan Ukraine, while still ruled essentially by a corrupt oligarchy, is geopolitically westward-leaning, and the Ukrainian political nation is being built on a clear anti-Russian foundation. Russia may control Donbass for the time being, and may keep Crimea for good, but the bulk of Ukraine has become a ward of the West. Ukraine's overall stability now depends not so much on defense from Russia as on Kiev's ability to deal with the hard-hit economy and deep-seated corruption.

Georgia, two of whose former provinces, Abkhazia and South Ossetia, have been recognized by Russia as independent states – with Russian garrisons in place in both – has recently maintained a calm relationship with Russia, with low border tensions and a revival of trade. In 2014, the EU concluded an association agreement with Georgia, and NATO reaffirmed its pledge to admit the country sometime in the future. Interestingly, in contrast to what happened in Ukraine, this did not evoke overly negative reactions from Moscow. To the

Kremlin, the current pro-Western but predictable government in Tbilisi led by the "Georgian Dream" coalition is much preferable to the regime of former President Mikheil Saakashvili, now governor of Ukrainian Odessa, whom Russia does not want to see back in power in Georgia.

In Moldova, the EU has been seeking to preserve the country's European orientation, despite periodic corruption scandals in the ruling coalition and the rise of pro-Russian opposition parties. For Moscow, however, Moldova's importance cannot be compared to that of Ukraine. The Kremlin is paying attention to the small impoverished country and is supporting its clients there, but it is not prepared to mount a major effort to draw Moldova into its orbit. However, Ukraine's decision in 2015 to ban Russian military transit to Transnistria, a separatist enclave which broke off from Moldova in 1990, has squeezed the small (1,500 men or so) Russian garrison in the area and raised fears of incidents. This is a latent conflict which should be closely watched, lest it creates another hot spot in Russian–Western relations.

To roll back traditional Russian influence in the Balkans, NATO in 2015 invited Montenegro to join, despite the unsavory reputation of its government – whose leader Milo Jukanovich has been in place for twenty-five years, longer than Belarus's Lukashenko

– and the less than enthusiastic support for membership among ordinary Montenegrins. The EU has also been managing an ever closer association with Serbia (Russia's main historical ally in the region) and Kosovo. Brussels essentially told Bulgaria, also known for long-standing ties with Russia, to withdraw from Gazprom's South Stream project. Western capitals monitored closely the flirtations with Moscow of Viktor Orbán's right-wing government in Hungary and Alexis Tsipras's left-wing Syriza cabinet in Greece, but eventually concluded that both are simply opportunistic. In any event, a campaign to rid South-Eastern Europe of remnants of Russian influence was in full evidence.

Information warfare

Information space, which despite the confrontation has essentially remained a global commons, has become a major battleground in the new Western–Russian rivalry. The Western mainstream media were virtually unanimous in strongly condemning Russia's violation of Ukraine's sovereignty in Crimea, the intervention in Donbass and the downing of the Malaysian plane, and were in wholesale repudiation of the Russian regime, its corruption and backward-looking ideological underpinnings, its cultural conservatism, and its neo-imperial ambitions backed by military force. As a result, the image of the Russian Federation in the West is now arguably worse than that of the communist Soviet Union in its heyday. Given such public attitudes, it was probably easier for US and British leaders to engage Joseph Stalin in the 1940s and Leonid Brezhnev in the 1970s than it is for their current successors to reach out to Vladimir Putin.

The Russian state-controlled media, for their part, have launched a most vitriolic campaign against the West, above all the United States. This campaign, too, has broken a few historical records. The disrespect and disdain accorded Vladimir Putin in the West is richly reciprocated by the Russian media depicting US and other Western leaders. Old taboos which were in effect during the Soviet period have been lifted. Apart from the invasion of Iraq, the bombing of Belgrade and the destruction of Libya, the United States stands accused of anything from plotting to dismember Russia to masterminding the Arab Spring to helping create al-Qaeda and ISIS. Arguably, this campaign can be stopped by the Kremlin at a moment's notice, but the longer it continues, the more of a mark it will leave on Russian people's minds.

Compared to stale Soviet propaganda, the products of the Russian state-owned media are of superior quality. The Kremlin may have created one of the most efficient and effective public information tools any government possesses in today's world. Its TV broadcasts are timely, vivid and often highly persuasive, at least for the Russian audience. Vladimir Putin owes part of his phenomenal popularity to Russian television reaching out to ordinary men and women in the country and communicating to them a narrative they believe. Mr Putin himself is an accomplished story-teller, capable of connecting to the bulk of his electorate. Again, unlike his Soviet forerunners, Putin succeeds in an open information space, where the rate of Internet penetration has reached 72 percent.

There can be no repeat of the high accomplishments of Western propaganda instruments during the Cold War, when, despite the Iron Curtain and the massive Soviet jamming of foreign broadcasts, the BBC, the Voice of America, Deutsche Welle, Radio Liberty and others had millions of listeners across the Soviet Union, who turned to them in search of reliable news and convincing explanations. BBC TV can be had on cable in major Russian cities; Radio Liberty has a studio in downtown Moscow; and VOA is freely available on the Internet. There is even a Russian government-supported web portal, Inosmi.ru, which publishes uncensored translations of all important articles in the Western media about Russia. Rather than hushing up criticism of Russia and its leaders, which the Soviet Union practiced all the time, the Russian state-run media attack this criticism immediately, head-on, and seek to demolish the Western story. Moscow is now not afraid of critical words and counters them with words and images of its own. Most Russians find this approach compelling.

This is one reason why Western counter-propaganda now targets not so much Russians in Russia itself as Russian speakers in the neighboring states, primarily the Baltic countries and Ukraine. The aim is to prevent them from becoming Russia's "fifth column" on the Western side of the new divide cutting through Europe. This is realistic: the paradox of the common information space is that the media environment in a given area is usually dominated by the prevailing local narrative.

Use of Western soft power

There are few illusions in the West that it can influence Russian domestic politics from the outside. This is not just the result of the measures taken by

Putin and his supporters beginning in 2012, such as the law which branded foreign-funded NGOs "foreign agents." The Russian elites, for all their wealth and familiarity with the West, are anything but pro-Western in their attitudes, outlook and ambitions. They are also closely tied to the Kremlin, with relatively few defectors. The Russian middle class is relatively small – even in happier times its share of the population was between 15 and 20 percent – and is currently shrinking, hard hit by the crisis. Much of it, moreover, is composed of government officials loyal to the state. The bulk of the Russian population at large – around two-thirds – are staunch Putin supporters. After Crimea, this fan club has swelled by another 20 percent. The pro-Western liberals, many of whom are strongly anti-Putin, are too few and far between, largely disunited and demoralized and, crucially, out of touch with the common people.

The hope of some in the West is that, in the war of values, soft power is their greatest asset. This soft power is most effective when it comes to such issues as peace and prosperity, affluence, prospects of a better future for the next generation, and the general quality of life. However, soft power is much more effective in attracting the more mobile elements in Russian society to emigrate to Europe or North America than in motivating the Russian people in Russia itself to embrace and practice Western values, not to speak of supporting Western policies. Even as the Russian people seek to deal with corruption, lawlessness, arbitrariness, rights abuse and monopolies of various sorts, it is not a given, to put it mildly, that a Russia which shares more values with Western countries will also align its interests with those of the United States or the EU.

Cooperation within confrontation

Western leaders recognize, of course, that it is wrong to see Russia only as a threat. The German chancellor, Angela Merkel, having taken a tough stance on Russian violations of the post-Cold War "peace order" in Europe, never stopped reminding others that fixing and maintaining security in Europe required cooperation, even partnership, with Russia. Berlin made it clear that it wanted the implementation of the Minsk II agreement as a prerequisite for normalizing relations between Germany and Russia. France's François Hollande and other EU leaders also subscribe to that view.

For the United States, the geopolitical importance

of Ukraine was never too high, and it waned when the armed conflict there abated. Washington, however, needed Moscow's assistance in 2015 to complete the nuclear deal with Iran, which – to the surprise of the White House – did not fall victim to the Ukraine crisis raging at the time. After Iran, the US needed Russia to try to reach a political settlement in Syria, and a degree of cooperation became possible. North Korea's experimentation with thermonuclear weapons also puts a premium on US–Russian collaboration.

To those fearful of Russia, these elements of cooperation constitute "appeasement" or even amount to a "betrayal" of a principled Western stance. In reality, national interests continue to prevail. The United States and the EU countries will reach out to Russia when they have to – and when they believe that the degree of commonality of interest is sufficient to expect productive collaboration. This, however, does not represent either appeasement or betrayal. Contemporary Western–Russian relations are highly competitive on account of the fundamental clash of interests regarding the global and regional order, and any cooperation between the parties will happen within the wider environment of continued confrontation.

US and EU responses to the Russian challenge

suggest that they regard the challenge as real but moderate, manageable primarily by economic means. This may appear reasonable, but it misses the central issue: if the sanctions and other measures fail to bring Russia back into line, how then should the West relate to a major power which rejects the Western-dominated order and shares that attitude with other even more powerful non-Western countries.

4

Navigating the New Normal

To begin with, one needs to recognize that, as time goes by, the West's challenges related to Russia are not going away or getting smaller. A stronger Russia, should it emerge, will be a stronger challenger; but a weaker and, particularly, a failing Russia will be an even more formidable challenge to deal with. One also needs from the start to drop any residual illusions about a Russia somehow reassociated with the West and more or less following its lead. That window is permanently closed.

Russia looks ossified, even petrified, under the current leadership, which has been in place for over a decade and a half. Yet, it will change, either more smoothly, as a result of policies from above interacting with processes from below, or perhaps abruptly, in unexpected ways and without much prior warning, as it has done a couple of times in its modern history. However, even as Russia changes, it will be different from the West and even from its neighbors in Central Europe such as Poland. Russia will act in its own way and will not be subject to Western-designed norms and conventions in either domestic or international behavior.

Russia will continue to compete with the West. The West's hope that Russia will inevitably succumb to the pressure of economic factors, such as the low oil price and economic sanctions, resulting also in the lack of investment and a ban on technology transfers, is so far just a hope. Even if Russia continues on a downward path, this descent may be long and will not necessarily lead to a friendlier policy vis-à-vis the West. The opposite is at least as likely. Pro-Western political and social forces within Russia are at their weakest in decades. Popular Russian nationalism defines itself as frankly anti-Western.

Competition and rivalry is not all there is to the West's relationship with Russia. There are compelling reasons for cooperation in a few selected areas. As already mentioned, in the field of WMD non-proliferation, Moscow has continued to interact productively with Washington and others on Iran and North Korea, despite the general atmosphere of US–Russian confrontation. In Syria, Russia is key to the future political and military developments.

Over time, Russia may have to become more involved in Afghanistan and Central Asia in order to oppose armed radicals there. Up to a point, its interests will be aligned with those of the West. With Islamist extremism a rising threat to Russia itself, Moscow will continue to fight terrorism both within its own borders and internationally. The transnational nature of contemporary terrorism makes Moscow a valuable partner to Western governments, whatever they think about Putin or his regime.

Thus, Russia in the foreseeable future will be primarily a competitor but may also occasionally – and within the general environment of competition – be a partner of the West. Under the present politico-economic system, it is likely to continue on a declining trajectory, but its military power will grow for the time being. This unequal mix of competition and cooperation, economic decline and military expansion, will make crafting a Western policy toward Russia a particularly difficult task. This task can be divided into elements, each with its own time horizon.

Taking risk-reduction measures

In the short term, the focus has to be on ensuring that the West's relations with Russia do not get out of control and lead to a dangerous collision that no one wants. The conflict in Ukraine's east is now undergoing a lull, but it may be reignited and expand beyond the present battlefield. The number one priority is to make sure that it is safely controlled. It is too much to expect the West to pressure Ukraine into implementing Minsk II, which Kiev hates and Moscow likes. The least bad way under the circumstances would be to build a firewall around the zone of conflict to make sure that it does not spread.

It is also highly important to agree with Russia in avoiding any provocation involving Russian and US/NATO military assets and forces, in Europe and elsewhere. Accidents involving military aircraft and naval ships are particularly dangerous. It is also necessary to avoid provocative military exercises along the new line of the military stand-off on Russia's north-western borders in Europe. As such exercises will continue in the absence of conventional arms control in Europe, some transparency would help. The purpose of the exercises can only be conventional deterrence, as actual war-fighting between Russia and NATO would almost certainly lead to a nuclear catastrophe.

A related issue is military deployments. So far, NATO has abided by the terms of the Founding

Act on relations with Russia, which rules out large-scale military deployments and massive military infrastructure development in the eastern member countries. With Russia–NATO cooperation over, and relations downgraded virtually to Cold War levels, there is pressure building up to terminate the constraints and deploy substantial foreign (preferably US) forces and bases in the Baltic States and Poland. If this happens, the relationship between the West and Russia will become even more militarized, with Moscow probably seeking to counter Western conventional troop presence on its borders with a nuclear threat to the United States and its European allies.

This may also be Russia's reaction to the deployment of US ballistic missile defenses in Eastern Europe and East Asia, ostensibly to counter missile threats from Iran and North Korea. Even though the Russian nuclear deterrent will not lose its effectiveness in the foreseeable future, these US deployments will not be ignored. In the asymmetrical situation of the lack of military balance between Russia and NATO, Moscow will have to rely more heavily on its strategic offensive systems. With traditional nuclear arms control between Washington and Moscow now history, it will be important for both sides at least to engage in a dialogue to help avoid erroneous assessment and resultant miscalculation.

This would require, at a minimum, keeping lines of communication open. Multilateral fora such as the UN Security Council, the NATO–Russia Council, and the Organization for Security and Cooperation in Europe will need to have a bigger role to play. The institutions which functioned during the Cold War should assume some of the familiar functions; the bodies built in the hope of cooperation would need to be transformed into platforms for managing conflict. It is important that dialogue in all these organizations is not stopped as punishment for Russian behavior or in protest at Western actions; rather, it is in the crisis periods that such bodies will be particularly, maybe critically, useful.

In an environment where top-level communications have virtually broken down and only transactional foreign policy is able to operate, it is highly desirable for small groups of trusted individuals from both sides, who enjoy the confidence of their national leaders as well as each other, to carry on with more broad-ranging dialogue on managing the adversarial relationship and organizing cooperative projects where the parties' interests approximate or coincide. These projects might range from the fight against extremism, to stemming radicalism, to the diplomatic process on crises such as Syria, to efforts to prevent WMD proliferation, and to less controversial issues such as dealing with infectious diseases and climate change.

Toward a new security arrangement in Europe and Greater Eurasia

In the medium and long term, it is necessary to work toward a new security arrangement in Europe and Greater Eurasia. The well-worn concept of European security needs to be rethought. By tradition, it was based on balances: initially among European states themselves, and later between the two blocs led by the United States and the Soviet Union. In the post-Cold War era an attempt was made to organize it around NATO, which was to expand to include virtually all of Europe except for Russia, which would be linked to the system by a special partnership arrangement. This attempt has failed, but there is no going back to the old bloc-based equilibrium. Russia has no real bloc to lead. Russia alone cannot balance NATO. However, the geopolitical framework has expanded beyond Europe.

Just as in the twentieth century European security expanded across the Atlantic, its twenty-first-century version also needs to expand, this time in the opposite direction to embrace all of Greater Eurasia. With China moving west toward Europe along its "One Belt, One Road" route, Russia looking toward Asia and the Middle East, and the United States repositioning itself with regard to both Asia and Europe, the security interests of the great powers across the entire continent of Eurasia are becoming more closely intertwined. Thus, twenty-first-century security arrangements will have to include China, as in the last century they came to include America. This expansion, however, is nothing like the Cold War situation when the United States came to the rescue of Western Europe. China is not coming to the rescue of a weakened Russia, and Eurasia is not becoming an area of intense Sino-American rivalry. The picture is more complex.

The transcontinental, transoceanic system which is emerging not just in Eurasia but in the northern hemisphere includes three great powers: the United States, China and Russia. It also includes a number of US allies that generally follow its lead but are powerful economically: the countries of the European Union, plus Japan, Turkey and South Korea. There is also a potential fourth great power,

India, whose might and ambitions will significantly expand over time, and there are a number of important regional players, such as Iran, Pakistan, Saudi Arabia and Indonesia.

To be minimally stable, the emerging system will need to rest on the basic principle of rough equilibrium among the great powers, some sort of balance between competing regional ones, and adequate protection to others. This will require creating a situation in which all key elements – i.e., great powers – are essentially satisfied that their security is not threatened by one or both of the other great powers. Regional powers would be safely balanced by their competitors or by the rest of the region. And all other countries would be sufficiently protected by means of alliances, partnerships and credible guarantees.

Although by far the weakest of the three great powers, Russia will play a pivotal role in that system. This follows from its geography, which reaches from Eastern and Northern Europe to East and Central Asia, and from the Arctic to the Caspian; from its natural and human resources; from its nuclear and conventional military power; and from its vast international experience as a European, Eurasian and global player over the course of many centuries. Of particular importance is Russia's strong determination to play solo, not being the junior partner or tributary state of anyone – in today's world, Washington or Beijing.

While Russia is pivotal – aligning itself with different players while always following its own self-interest – its role will not be central. The central stage will be occupied by the United States, seeking to protect and prolong its global dominance, and China, the rising challenger to that dominance. A Sino-Russian alliance is improbable for the same reason that the US–Russian one never came about: Moscow will not recognize the other partner's leadership, and the other partner would find Russia too difficult and ultimately unnecessary to humor. However, following the rupture between Russia and the West, the Sino-Russian rapprochement has reached the level of genuine entente that others need to take seriously.

China and Russia share an intense resentment of US global dominance. They both advocate a world order based on great-power equilibrium, although, while China dreams of a new kind of bipolarity, Russia is wedded to a "polycentric" system of several major players. Like Moscow, Beijing is adamantly opposed to a Western-supported spread of democracy and defends the existing political regime in the name of national sovereignty. Like Russia, China is seeking to dominate its neighborhood in the name of the national interest. It employs a strikingly different strategy from Russia's in Crimea and Ukraine, but it clearly regards Taiwan, the islands in the East China Sea and much of the South China Sea as its core interests. For Beijing, increasing its influence in the neighborhood and eventually across Eurasia is a key part of the strategy of China's global rise.

So far, in view of its evident limitations and potential for rivalry, the United States has been relaxed about the evolution of the Russian–Chinese relationship. This attitude, however, is overly complacent. Russia is not China's equal, but neither is it its satellite. In principle, under a different system of governance and management, and with an economic model that encourages development and innovation, it could marshal enough resources and unchain sufficient potential to become a formidable and effective player. Russia's decline is a reality, but whether this is terminal or temporary is an open question yet to be answered by the Russian people. In a number of key areas – military and foreign affairs, diplomacy, intelligence – Russia continues to be ahead of China. It does not have many allies, but it has pragmatically partnered with a number of countries, including India and Vietnam. Moscow has not written Tokyo off, and it keeps up a productive relationship with Seoul.

China and Russia are not going to clash over Central Asia, as some in the West have long been prophesying, and, while they will not build a formal alliance, Russia will be contributing to the growth of China's air and sea power. As the two militaries exercise together, Beijing and Moscow will continue cooperating closely on world order and regional security issues. As the competition between China and the United States grows more intense, what China can get from Russia will become more important. The strategic triangle of Washington, Beijing and Moscow has mutated over the past forty-plus years, but it has not vanished as some thought. However, it has lost its salient feature: Washington no longer dominates. It is Beijing which now has better relations with Washington and Moscow than the latter two have between themselves.

This situation challenges the West to come up with a broader strategic approach. To have any chance of acceptance, the transcontinental/ transoceanic security arrangement needs to be guided by the principles of politico-ideological pluralism and mutual respect. This will be a hard sell in the West and will probably result in the simultaneous preaching of values in public and a hard-nosed pursuit of interest in reality. The arrangement cannot be managed within a single overarching institution. Rather, better use will need to be made of the multiple existing institutions while ensuring better connectivity and interaction among them. Thus, the OSCE might find it useful to talk to the Shanghai Cooperation Organization (SCO); China could harmonize its "One Belt, One Road" project not only with the Eurasian Economic Union but also with the EU; and so on.

The Russia policy

In this broader picture, relations with Russia are but one, albeit important, element. Basically, the choice for the West in that relationship is between containment and engagement on mutually agreed terms. For now, containment is winning. Russia remains under pressure politically and economically. In the domain of public information, it is pictured as a rogue state led by a gang of criminal, corrupt, and even murderous figures. This approach, however, hinges on the expectation of Russia's inevitable decline and hopes of a political transformation that would return the country to the Western orbit which it left in the mid-2000s.

Dealing with a disintegrating Russia would again,

as twenty-five years ago in the case of the collapsing USSR, demand maximum attention to the issues of assuring nuclear security and preventing WMD proliferation. Much else could be borrowed from contemporary history books, but one key element will be missing: unlike in the final days of the Soviet Union and the first days of the new Russian Federation, the West will have few friends in the Kremlin or among the Russian elites, whether outgoing or incoming. It would also have to deal with a population which would blame their woes largely on malicious Western policies.

And, very important, since a disintegrating Russia would present a major danger to China, Beijing can be expected to play a key role in preventing Russia's collapse. While the end of the Soviet Union presented a historic chance to the West, which it chose not to use, a severely weakened Russia could become an opportunity to China to reach out and help it recover, so as to make a claim on its resources and exercise long-term influence on its policies. Should this happen, the geopolitical axis of Eurasia would shift.

This, however, is not necessarily what the future holds. As demonstrated in chapter 3, some Western policies, such as sanctions, can be and are counter-productive. Russia's current economic model is unsustainable, and its governance is appalling. Russia is in deep crisis, which can be likened to a severe illness. However, as is common in such cases, if the patient does not die, he will get stronger. If Russia goes down and disintegrates again, the West will be presented with one set of problems; if it recovers, the challenge will be bigger than it is now.

A Russia which has recovered and set out on a path of economic and technological development would be of interest to European business circles. Investments would again become profitable, and the Russian market of 145 million consumers would look more attractive. At some point, some sanctions would have to be eased or even lifted. There would be no emergence of a Greater Europe from Lisbon to Vladivostok, but some form of relationship between the European Union and the Eurasian Economic Union would make sense after the latter has survived the test of the present economic crisis. This would not make Russia "part of Europe," but it might eventually lead to the two becoming partners in selected areas.

An economically stronger Russia would make its foreign policy even more effective. Russia has made a difference even when it was weak but punching above its weight. If it becomes stronger, it will make much more of a difference. With both its own integration into the West and the former Russian provinces' integration into a Greater Russia no longer viable options, a Russia which is a single major nation-state, global in its outlook and interacting with all its neighbors in Greater Eurasia – the EU, China, India, Japan, South-East Asia and the Middle East – plus others elsewhere, could be an influential world player. The West should also be prepared for this outcome, no matter how unlikely it may seem at the moment.

Dealing with a stronger Russia, but one which no longer sees itself as part of the Euro-Atlantic community – which was Moscow's official policy line as recently as six years ago – will not be easy. Competition, if anything, will intensify. Russia's main goal at the global level is the establishment of a polycentric world order which would end the centuries-old domination of the West and cut short the second American century. In pursuit of this goal, Russia would broadly align itself with China, India, Brazil, Iran and a number of other non-Western countries.

Such an alignment would not result in permanent coalitions built around such fora as BRICS or SCO. There are serious issues within the non-West, not least between China and India. Moscow and Beijing do not always see eye to eye, and they have a host of practical issues to sort out in addition to some historical baggage. The non-West is not going to evolve into anything like the present-day West, a homogeneous community of like-minded nations with a set of shared values and undisputed leadership provided by the United States. Yet, with the addition of Russia from 2014, this group has gained a particularly combative great power.

The "new normal" of competition and even confrontation will last years. It might end sooner if the Russian Federation breaks down under the pressure of rivalry, like the Russian Empire did in the midst of World War I. The West would then have to deal with the consequences of another major collapse following that of the Soviet Union twenty-five years ago. There is no guarantee that it would be as relatively orderly and peaceful as the dismantlement of the USSR.

The competition might last longer if Russia is lucky enough to avoid a cataclysmic scenario but still lacks the will to begin improving its economy and overall governance. Then the West would be dealing with a country which would be simultaneously declining economically yet still able to marshal sufficient resources in the military sector to ensure its own security and pursue an active foreign policy, defying US global dominance.

In the seemingly unlikely but not totally impossible scenario of Russia using its confrontation with the world's most powerful country to diversify and modernize its economy, overhaul and upgrade its scientific and technological base, and radically improve governance at all levels – particularly by means of prizing competence and reducing corruption – it may become an even more formidable competitor with the West. In other words, a successfully modernized Russia would not again seek to join the West but, rather, press it harder to protect its interests and promote its own worldview. Whatever Russia's future, the conflict with the West is helping shape it.

Conclusion:
How Conflict with the West
Impacts on Russia

Over the centuries, Russia's relations with the West have been a combination of a desire to emulate the more advanced nations of Europe, and to learn from them, and an effort to preserve its own identity and provide security vis-à-vis Europe's hegemonic powers – and, more recently, the United States and its NATO allies. For periods of time, Russia dominated much of Central and Eastern Europe and was both the policeman of the continent and the hegemonic oppressor of other countries' freedom. The end of the twentieth century witnessed an unprecedented attempt by post-imperial Russia to join the West, become an integral part of it, and be accepted as a major Western power, second only, but not subservient to the United States. This one-of-a-kind adventure, however, has ended in failure.

Russia shares the blame for the way this has

116

ended. The Kremlin has blundered its way into the disaster in Ukraine: first by believing that Ukraine could be integrated into the Eurasian Union project, then by mistaking the Maidan for a US-hatched plot, and finally by embarking on the "Novorossia" misadventure. It has recklessly gambled with the goodwill of the Europeans, above all the Germans, bought at a very high price at the end of the Cold War and carefully sustained for a quarter-century after that. Putin's misreading of the German reaction to Crimea was stunning. Finally, Moscow's rupture with the West put it in an awkward position of overreliance on China, an unsentimental would-be superpower that, like the United States, does not regard Russia as its equal. Such "Realpolitik" does not serve the Russian national interest at all.

The present confrontation between Russia and the West is just two years old, but the rift is getting deeper by the week. This confrontation is highly asymmetrical. In all relevant areas, the power of the United States, not to speak of the West as a whole, exceeds that of Russia by the widest margin. The Kremlin genuinely fears US-designed, US-sponsored and US-directed "color revolutions." The Russian security community fears Western spying and its penetration of Russian officialdom and elites. The General Staff is concerned about the movement of NATO infrastructure toward Russia's borders, the US ballistic missile defenses, and strategic non-nuclear systems.

Many of these fears are groundless or overblown. NATO has certainly refocused on Russia and is now busy organizing new defenses. A nuclear superpower like Russia, however, has every reason to be confident about the power and effectiveness of its ultimate deterrent. Surprise invasions and decapitating strikes against Russia are prohibitively risky, and neutralizing its nuclear systems by means of ballistic missile defense will be out of the question for several decades to come. Similarly, a non-nuclear strike against Russia's strategic assets can never achieve adequate success to protect the attacker against Moscow's retaliation.

Thus, Russia has no serious reason to fear the West. Contrary to some popular inventions, the United States has no intention of breaking the Russian Federation into pieces and taking over the "juicier" parts. Western Europeans generally harbor no ill will toward Russia. Japan will not seek the return of the South Kuril Islands by force, and Canada will not attack Russian possessions in the Arctic. Poland, the Baltic States and Romania will remain frankly hostile and Britain and Sweden highly skeptical toward it, but none of these countries can mount a credible threat. Erdoğan's Turkey, of course, is a country to watch, but Russia has a range of assets to prevent or contain the threat of a direct collision.

Russia, however, cannot afford to take the present confrontation/alienation lightly. Moscow's breakout from the post-Cold War order carries a high price, to be paid over a long period of time. It cannot hope to defeat its former partners turned adversaries, but it can either use the stand-off as a challenge to improve its own ways or else succumb to it and seal its downward socio-economic and political trajectory. In the past two years, the Kremlin has been managing the situation while keeping the fundamentals of the politico-economic system intact. So far, it has shown neither a plan nor much of a desire to come up with a model that would encourage economic development and support entrepreneurship and innovation in the country.

If this continues much longer, it will be bad, and potentially tragic for the country. In the present situation of long-term confrontation with the West the consequences could be dire. Like World War I, which began with an apparent surge of Russian patriotism and support for the Romanov dynasty but finished off the empire and the dynasty within three years, the present conflict with the West, which started exactly a century later, has the potential to bring latent domestic tensions to a head. Russia is not a country where leaders are changed every four, five or six years by means of a ballot box, but it is a fact that in the last century the Russian people brought down the entire Russian state twice. The last such cataclysmic event occurred twenty-five years ago.

Russia's present crisis is the worst since the collapse of the Soviet Union, with the future as difficult to foresee. In contrast to that of Gorbachev, Putin's foreign policy is unlikely to grow more conciliatory as the crisis worsens, but the post-Putin era will probably provide a repudiation of many of the current practices, including in foreign policy. Russia, of course, will stay Russia: it will not attempt a new "docking" with Europe, but it may look for accommodation with it and with other neighbors. Such accommodation can only be shallow, given the differences in political, social, economic and values systems, but it might be sufficient to defuse many of the current risks. As a result, Russia's Realpolitik may become more realistic.

Whereas the challenge to the West regarding Russia is essentially a foreign policy issue, the challenge facing Russia in its stand-off with the West is overwhelmingly a domestic one. The real battlefield for Moscow is neither Ukraine nor Syria, but Russia itself. How Moscow manages the crisis and whether it succeeds in putting the country on a development trajectory will crucially depend on the Russian elites. So far, they have been found lacking. The question is whether they can rise to the challenge of relaunching the Russian economy. Should they fail, Russia's future certainly looks bleak.

Further Reading

There is a small library of literature on present-day Russia and its foreign policy. Much of it is devoted to the person of Vladimir Putin. Quite a few books are obviously polemical, and many are superficial. I will supply the reader with a reasonably short list of titles, which, I should add, with just one exception, depict the difficult relationship between Russia, on the one hand, and the United States and Europe, on the other, from a Western standpoint.

Serious works on the issue of relations between Russia and the West include Georgetown University Professor Angela Stent's treatise on the US–Russian relations, *The Limits of Partnership: US–Russian Relations in the Twenty-First Century* (Princeton University Press, 2014), which appeared on the eve of the Ukraine crisis, and Columbia University Professor Emeritus Robert Legvold's *Return to Cold War* (Polity, 2016).

Specifically on this seminal crisis, I would recommend *Conflict in Ukraine: The Unwinding of the Post-Cold*

Further Reading

War Order, by Lehigh University's Rajan Menon and my Carnegie colleague Eugene Rumer (MIT Press, 2015); Kent University Professor Richard Sakwa's *Frontline Ukraine: Crisis in the Borderlands* (I. B. Tauris, 2015); British researcher Andrew Wilson's *Ukraine Crisis: What it Means for the West*; and veteran journalist and Brookings scholar Marvin Kalb's *Imperial Gamble: Putin, Ukraine, and the New Cold War* (Brookings Institution Press, 2015).

On the wider issue of Moscow's foreign policy, I would recommend Andrei P. Tsygankov's *Russia's Foreign Policy: Change and Continuity in National Identity* (4th edn, Rowman & Littlefield, 2016) and Jeff Mankoff's *Russian Foreign Policy: the Return of Great Power Politics* (Rowman & Littlefield, 2011). Another notable recent contribution to the body of research is Nicolas Gvosdev and Christopher Marsh's *Russian Foreign Policy: Interests, Vectors, and Sectors* (Sage, 2014).

Great background reading is Dominic Lieven's *Empire: The Russian Empire and its Rivals* (Yale University Press, 2001); Walter Laqueur's *Putinism: Russia and its Future with the West* (Thomas Dunne, 2015); and Charles Clover's *Black Wind, White Snow: The Rise of Russia's New Nationalism* (Yale University Press, 2016).

Notes

1 Robert Gates, *Duty: Memoirs of a Secretary at War*. New York: Alfred Knopf, 2014, p. 157.

2 Ibid., pp. 157–8.

3 Ibid., pp. 157, 167.

4 Remarks by the US secretary of defense Ashton Carter at the Economic Club, Washington, DC, February 2, 2016.

5 Karl Marx and Frederick Engels, *Collected Works*. Moscow: Partizdat, 1936, Vol. XVI, Part II, pp. 3–40.

6 Norman Davies, preface to Edward Lucas, *The New Cold War*. New York: Palgrave Macmillan, 2008, p. xii.

7 Hillary Clinton, *Hard Choices*. New York: Simon & Schuster, 2014, pp. 236–43.

8 Henry Kissinger, *Diplomacy*. New York: Simon & Schuster, 1994, p. 815.

9 Davies, preface, p. xiii.

Notes

10 Remarks by the US secretary of defense Ashton Carter at the Economic Club, Washington, DC, February 2, 2016.